Handley Page
HALIFAX
PORTFOLIO

Compiled by
R.M. Clarke

ISBN 0 948 207 892

Published by Brooklands Books in conjunction with

A BROOKLANDS AIRCRAFT PORTFOLIO

Portfolios in preparation will cover: Spitfire, Lancaster, Wellington, P51 Mustang etc.
Cover Photography by Charles E. Brown/Raf Museum

DISTRIBUTED BY

Motorbooks International
Osceola
Wisconsin 24020
USA

Brooklands Book Distribution Ltd
Holmerise, Sevenhills Road
Cobham, Surrey KT11 1ES
England

A BROOKLANDS AIRCRAFT PORTFOLIO

A BROOKLANDS AIRCRAFT PORTFOLIO

This is the first of a new series of books covering classic World War Two aircraft, compiled from contemporary material originally published in Flight, The Aeroplane and Aircraft Production. We have combed through wartime volumes of these journals and selected representative features on these famous fighting aircraft, covering every aspect of each aeroplane: genealogies, technical appraisals, handling characteristics, combat and operational reports and so forth. In addition to a wealth of photographs each book contains one or more contemporary cutaway drawings, for which both Flight and The Aeroplane were noted. These articles have not been edited in any way and are straight, high-quality reprints from the original issues. In addition to this wealth of contemporary material further features have been reprinted from Aeroplane Monthly, successor to The Aeroplane, written with hindsight by pilots, engineers and crewmen who knew their aircraft intimately, inside and out.

Whether or not you flew in these aircraft, this series conveys, in a unique form, the character and background of aircraft that fought for peace during six long years of war.

If you enjoy this book you will surely enjoy others in this series.

Richard Riding
Editor
Aeroplane Monthly

Printed in Hong Kong

HALIFAX

First Details of One of Great Britain's New "Heavies": Formidable Offensive and Defensive Armament

(Illustrated by " Flight " Photographs)

An historic occasion : Lady Halifax christens the machine by breaking a bottle of champagne on its nose.

WHEN Lady Halifax christened one of the new Handley Page four-engined bombers last week, she christened not merely one aircraft, but a whole family, for, as the enemy knows from experience, these machines have already wrought havoc on German and Italian targets. As Lord Halifax said in a speech before the christening ceremony, there is an old Yorkshire prayer: "From Hull, Hell and Halifax deliver us," and the time is coming when the enemy may well come to echo the latter part of that sentiment.

It was not until the Halifax was wheeled out of the hangar after the christening that one could form any real opinion of the new bomber. The writer was irresistibly reminded of a day during the last war, when the Handley Page 0/400 was similarly wheeled out of its hangar at Hendon and subsequently flown. It is no detriment to the Halifax to say that that first view of the 0/400 was more impressive. One had never seen an aeroplane comparable in size, and thus there was an element of awe which, somehow was absent when the

tractor brought the Halifax out on to the aerodrome. And yet the new four-engined bomber is as far ahead of the types to which we have now been accustomed.

At first one is puzzled by this absence of awe. But as one walks around the machine and inspects it in more detail, one realises that the "ordinariness," if the expression may

After the ceremony : Mr. Handley Page discusses the bomber with Lord Halifax. On the left Lady Halifax is talking to Mr. S. R. Worley, chairman of Handley Page, Ltd., and on the right are seen Mrs. Handley Page and Lord Sempill.

Impressive size : The man under the wing lends scale to the picture above, and other views indicate general features and the manoeuvrability which has been so well combined with size in the Halifax.

be forgiven, is due to the excellent lines and proportions of the aircraft. Not until men are seen near it does one realise the size. We have no idea who laid out the general outline, but whoever it was deserves great credit. The Halifax *looks* right, and, judging by the manner in which Mr. Talbot, the firm's test pilot, " threw it about," it *is* right. We gather from Mr. Handley Page that the Halifax is one of those rare aeroplanes which were right from the very beginning. When that happens, the result is always very much better than any that can be obtained by modifications of the original design. In the case of the Halifax, the only "mod." of any importance was a slight shifting of the rudder hinges.

Of the performance and bomb load nothing may be said, but when Mr. Talbot flew across the aerodrome at full speed, and only a few feet up, it was not difficult for the experienced to make a very shrewd guess at the top speed. The combination of range and bomb load could not be so easily estimated ; but it is good, of that there is no doubt. The cleanness of the aerodynamic design is obvious, and with four Rolls-Royce Merlins on a span of 99ft. the wing, of fairly high aspect ratio, is not unduly split up. Nose and tail turrets, too, have been

HALIFAX

worked into the design in such a way as to interfere but little with the air-flow.

On the day of the demonstration, Mr. Talbot did a down-wind take-off. The Handley Page slotted trailing-edge flaps appear to be very effective in giving, at one position, great increase of lift without much increase of drag.

Structurally the Halifax is, needless to say, of all-metal construction. The Handley Page system of breaking down the structure into a number of units has been followed, and the resulting production rate is most gratifying.

Reference has already been made to the good shape of the forward and aft gun turrets. Even the "bay window" for the bomb aimer does not spoil the nose, as may be seen from the photographs. His view is, of course, very good indeed, as it that of the pilot, whose cockpit is ahead of the engines. Owing to the fact that the leading edge is swept back, the outer engines are set back in relation to the inner engines, and so the lateral view extends abaft of the beam.

Nothing may be said of the internal layout of the Halifax, but it has been designed for comfort as well as utility, and a very effective cabin-heating arrangement is incorporated. Access to the tail is particularly easy, owing to the great depth of the fuselage.

Troubles due to ice formation have not been overlooked, and the tail of the Halifax is equipped with a de-icer. The Rotol airscrews have also received attention, but one would have expected to find other parts of the aircraft guarded against this danger.

Altogether the new Handley Page Halifax is a worthy addition to our growing air strength, and the work which the type has already accomplished places it among the most formidable of our new heavy types. The 0/400 came too late to bomb Berlin in the last war. This time neither Berlin nor many other German cities will avoid the destructive powers of its modern counterpart.

The Merlin engines of the Halifax are staggered, the inner engines being forward of the outer. The airscrews are Rotol. Note front gunner's turret, supplemented by the rear turret shown in the view below.

In the three-quarter rear view can be seen the Handley Page slotted flaps, which improve the take-off by giving extra lift with little increase of drag.

FRIEND or FOE?

Four-engined Rivals with Twin Tails

HANDLEY-PAGE HALIFAX. Gun turret in tail; rudders divided by fixed tailplane tips; vertical surfaces outrigged. Fixed tail-wheel.

I N recent utterances, in print and on the radio, a number of eminent gentlemen have reminded us —though probably we didn't need it —that should the Germans succeed in their Russian objective before the real winter sets in, then an attempted invasion of this country next spring will be a foregone conclusion.

Be that as it may, however, it is certainly pretty safe to assume that, if and when the invasion of this country is attempted, air-borne troops will play a big part, and enemy troop-carriers of types perhaps not previously seen over these shores may well be pressed into service. It will be just as well, therefore, if we can identify them before they deposit their hostile occupants, especially when, as exemplified by the illustrations on this page, they resemble some current British type.

Similarity

The similarity between the Halifax and the Junkers Ju 90 troop transport is particularly marked from this angle. One gets the full benefit of the short outboard engine nacelles and the long inner pair with the retracted wheels protruding, and at the same time the violent backsweep on the leading-edge of the Junkers' wing is minimised, while the shape of the nose is almost entirely hidden.

Their respective tail groups are also very much alike, but the one important and obvious difference is provided by the rear turret of the British bomber. The "chisel" extremity of the Ju fuselage boasts no sting.

Both tailplanes taper slightly (the Halifax on the leading-edge only), and are set in approximately the same

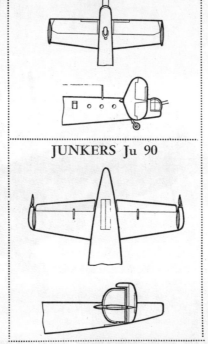

HALIFAX I

JUNKERS Ju 90

position in relation to the fuselage. But the mounting of the fins and rudders provides an exception to the usual national characteristic in that, this time, it is the German machine, not the British, on which the tailplane tips project outside the vertical surfaces. Notice, too, that the projecting tip is streamlined off by a piece of fairing attached to the outer surface of the rudder, which also has a horn balance. The rudder surfaces of the Halifax are also unusual in that each one is divided by the flush-fitting tailplane tip, the elevators being "inset" portions of the fixed horizontal structure. In the case of the Ju 90, however, the fixed tailplane and the fixed fins have the same chord where they intersect, the elevators being projecting surfaces shelved off at the outer corners to permit rudder movement.

Another little difference worth noting is that the Junkers' tail wheel completely retracts within the fuselage, whereas that of the Halifax does not.

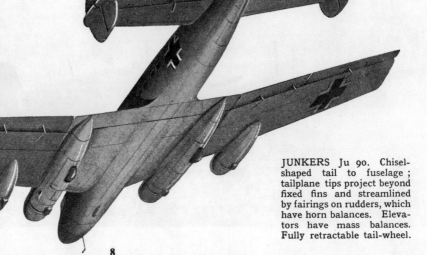

JUNKERS Ju 90. Chisel-shaped tail to fuselage; tailplane tips project beyond fixed fins and streamlined by fairings on rudders, which have horn balances. Elevators have mass balances. Fully retractable tail-wheel.

Halifax Squadron

The New Handley Page in Service : Its Size, Comfort and Convenience :
Successful Start to Its Career

HALIFAX TRIO : A view looking aft from the front gun turret showing first pilot at the controls, radio operator below and the second pilot who normally sits alongside the first pilot.

THE year 1941 has seen the big four-engined bomber come into regular use by the R.A.F. Bomber Command. It is not a new policy but a new development. These monsters—for so we now regard them, though a few years hence they may seem as trifling as we now consider the Southampton flying boat, which was once consistently described in the daily papers as a "giant aircraft"—are certainly expensive to build and expensive in man-hours; but in maintenance and operation they are economical in man-power and pay good dividends in the weight of bombs which they unload on enemy targets for a given amount of effort. Their range brings within the danger area many targets which could formerly congratulate themselves on their immunity. As the number of such machines in use by the Bomber Command increases (as it is steadily doing) many of those distant targets may expect more frequent visits and more widespread destruction.

The sight of the new large bombers naturally sends the minds of older men back to the final stages of the last war, when the Handley Page O/400 was a new and astonishing machine. Those who had seen the first specimens to go into service sometimes told their friends that it was so big that "it frightened you." So it seems only natural and appropriate that the same firm which produced the O/400, the first large machine which any country (except Tsarist Russia) possessed, should be represented in the most recent stage of development by the four-engined Halifax. Of course. there is a great deal of difference between the old braced biplane with fabric-covered wings and fuselage and the new mid-wing cantilever monoplane of all-metal construction.

The Halifax is a bomber which immediately attracts the eye. It looks good, for it is a shapely aircraft for all its size. Briefly, its span is 99ft., its length 70ft., and its height 22ft. The top line of the fuselage is straight, but the line underneath is curved. The plan of the wings is rectangular to just beyond the two inboard engines, and from there they taper almost symmetrically, but more markedly on the trailing edge, to the square wing tips. The main wheels retract backwards. The engines are Rolls-Royce Merlins, and the airscrews are three-bladed and fully feathering.

It is most impressive to see the bomb-doors open and to realise the tremendous weight of destructive power which can be accommodated, but details of the bomb load would be information which the enemy would very much like to know, and therefore may not be given at present. Enemy factories have already had some taste of its quality, and it is understood that they have not enjoyed it.

Inside the Halifax one is surprised by the amount of space. One can stand up and walk about easily, and there is no awkward spot where one has to crawl on hands and knees, as in some earlier bombers. This makes for efficiency in operations, and incidentally would make it less difficult to move a wounded man on to the seat where he could lie and receive first-aid. This seat is situated centrally and during take-off the crew can sit on it together. The normal crew is seven.

The Crew's Stations

The stations for the crew in flight are rather unusual. The flight engineer (a new R.A.F. trade) sits in a compartment behind the pilots' cockpit underneath the astro-hatch, and now is trained to take observations, which are passed on to the navigator. The latter and the wireless operator have their station below the first pilot's seat. Down below them is the position for the bomb-aimer, while in the nose is the forward gun turret. These three latter positions are reached by moving aside the seat of the second pilot. A door cuts off the rear portion of the fuselage to exclude draught. The rear gun turret—aptly termed by our American friends the "stinger" turret—can be seen in the illustrations. Near the door is another sort of seat or bunk, which is not normally used as such in flight, but provides some comfort to the guard who sleeps in the machine when it is on the ground.

As is usual in large aircraft, the forward turret has two Browning machine-guns and the tail turret has four. The Halifax, in fact, can make it exceedingly unpleasant for intrusive enemy fighters, and some have already paid the penalty.

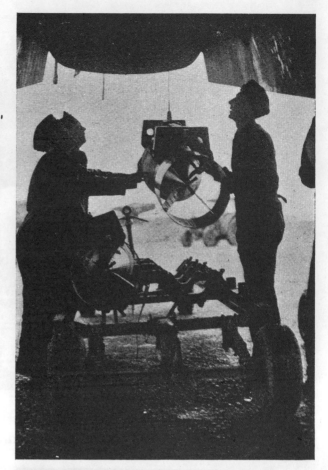

GOING TO RACK AND RUIN : Loading up the bomb racks of a Halifax. The bomb load and its variations are not for publication.

A very important point about a long-range bomber is the comfort of the crew. The whole of the Halifax is very well warmed, except for the nose and tail gun turrets. The rear gunner wears electrically heated clothes and part of

OH, MASTER, WE ARE SEVEN : The crew of a Halifax is made up of flight engineer, first and second pilots, wireless operator, navigator-bomb-aimer and two air gunners.

his protection includes a Brynzie vest made of silk netting, of about 1in. mesh, made of material similar to that of the shroud lines of a parachute. This is said to have especial virtue in keeping the body warm.

Another device inside the Halifax which attracted notice is a hatch opening on to the top of the fuselage, with a ladder of wire cable leading up to it. This is used by aircraftmen to get out on top when the machine is on the ground.

Like all modern bombers, the Halifax inside is a perfect magazine of flares and other items of equipment. The arrangement of the oxygen apparatus is particularly good and is a great improvement on that of some older types. It is easier to work, and avoids risk of leakages of the precious vapour. Naturally it takes a crew some little time to learn their way about and to know exactly where everything is, so as to be able to go to the right spot for it without hesitation. Crew members who have served in Whitleys go for a conversion course on a Halifax before being posted to a squadron which uses this new type. A pilot must have done a certain minimum number of trips in a Whitley as captain of the aircraft before he is considered eligible to be included as pilot in a Halifax crew. The Halifax is popular with the pilots, who find it easy to fly. It is very manœuvrable, which is a great advantage when avoiding *flak* or attacks by fighters.

The Halifax in Action

As official communiqués have told, this new bomber has already made itself felt in numerous raids over enemy territory. It almost goes without saying that it has bombed Bremen and Wilhelmshaven, but the full list of the targets which it has reached is a long one. It includes Berlin, Magdeburg, Mannheim, Essen, Kiel, Stettin, Hamburg, Karlsruhe, Cologne, Dusseldorf, Hanover, Frankfort and Duisberg. Its bombs have spread havoc in the Royal Arsenal at Turin, and the crews much enjoyed the trip over the Alps on both the outward and the return journeys.

One of the greatest, perhaps the greatest adventure in which a formation of Halifax bombers was concerned was the great daylight attack on La Pallice, when the *Scharnhorst* had sneaked off there from Brest. It was bound to be a daring affair, and losses were to be expected, but the object of the raid was to help in winning the Battle of the Atlantic.

R.A.F. bomber crews are never held back by considerations of possible losses, and doubtless as these men made their runs up on to the target they thought that if the *Scharnhorst* were to get loose again she might sink hundreds of tons of British shipping, cost the lives of hundreds of British seamen, and prevent the delivery of large supplies of munitions and food to Britain. At any rate they went in.

During the visit of a *Flight* representative to the station where a Halifax squadron lives, men who had taken part in this fine action described what happened. One said that as their machine approached La Pallice, and was only a few miles off, the bomb-aimer exclaimed "Target sighted," and at once a tense silence prevailed all through the machine every man waiting anxiously for the words "Bombs gone." Then the strain seemed to relax and they resumed their usual activities.

A gunner officer related how he was put in charge of the defence of his machine, after the bombing, to guide the machine back out of the danger zone. He took up his position under the astro-hatch, keeping his eye skinned for fighters up above, while the gunners at each end looked out for enemies below. This officer was, for the time, in command, and the captain of the aircraft obeyed his directions. There were swarms of Messerschmitts in the sky, perhaps 50 or 60 of them, and most of them were of the 109F mark. As each launched its attack, this officer shouted directions to the captain, and evasive action would throw the fighters off their mark. It must have been exciting work, and it required very nice judgment, but it was

TO KEEP HIS END UP : A Halifax rear gunner in his four-gun turret.

coolly and skilfully carried out. As a result his machine got home with only six bullet holes in it. The fighters pursued them in vain for as long as their petrol allowed, but finally drew off and returned to their bases.

As is well known, the enemy gave up hopes of getting the *Scharnhorst* away to a dockyard in the south and brought her back to Brest, where she received further attention from night-bombers. The whole country owes a big debt of gratitude to the men and the machines who carried through this fine attack.

Still more Halifax bombers will soon be added to Bomber Command, and perhaps they may be even more formidable as the result of the experience gained through the operations of the forerunners. *Caveat hostis* !

New Uses for Old Journals

WE are grateful to the many readers who have helped us to minimise the inconvenience caused by the restricted circulation imposed upon us by the shortage of paper. We have ample evidence that copies of *Flight* are passed from hand to hand, and that the last man to get them studies them as eagerly as his more fortunate fellows. But even an old copy of *Flight* is not by any means useless, and it is worth while to take a little trouble over the disposal of it by the reader who is last to receive it.

Waste paper is urgently needed for munitions, and readers of *Flight* may like to feel that even when copies have reached that stage, they can continue to help in the war work. One copy will not seem of great importance, but, rather surprisingly, it only takes about 6,500 copies of an average issue to make up a ton; and a ton of waste paper will make, for example, 71,000 of those little dust covers which are used to plug small openings of various sorts in aero engines. The shells fired from aircraft cannon are packed in boxes, and a ton of paper will make 3,000 of them.

So don't throw away your old *Flights* or other journals. See that they are collected by your local council and put to a useful purpose.

The HALIFAX

A Heavy Bomber with Great Load-carrying Capacity : Same Wing Area as H.P. O/400 of 1915, but 60,000 lb. Loaded Weight Instead of 14,000, and More Than Three Times the Speed

(Illustrated with Exclusive "Flight" Sketches and Photographs)

DURING the war 1914-18 Mr. F. Handley Page delivered a lecture to the Royal Aeronautical Society and stated—very ably, as one might expect of this British pioneer of aircraft design—the case for the large machine. In those days we had all become rather imbued with the idea, sound enough in itself in that it was based upon a fundamental law, that the percentage of structure weight increased rapidly with aircraft size. The law, quite briefly, is that whereas wing area increases proportionately as the square of the wing span, the weight increases as the cube. The law is known as the cube law, and presupposes geometric similarity ; that is to say that not only must the external shape of the aircraft remain the same, on the larger scale, but the components of the internal structure must be in every way to scale also, and must be made of the same materials.

What Mr. Handley Page did in his lecture was not to disprove the validity of the cube law, which is an obvious fundamental truth, but to point out that there are many ways in which the cube law can be "cheated." In a small aircraft there are a great many structural components which cannot be made as thin and light as the loads in them demand ; they would be too flimsy for handling, or they would need so much additional stiffening to make them rigid enough that their manufacture would become too slow and costly. In other words, "refinements" became possible which would be out of the question in small aircraft. The audience at that memorable lecture was impressed, but still slightly sceptical, although Mr. Handley Page was not merely talking

theory, for he had built the H.P. O/400, a large biplane of 100ft. span and 1,480 sq. ft. of wing area.

Since those early days the Handley Page Company has built many large aircraft ; the O/400 was followed by the still larger V/1500, and then by smaller bombers such as the Hyderabad, the Hinaidi, the Heyford, the Harrow, the Hampden, and now the much larger Halifax.

The Halifax is the first four-engined bomber produced by the Handley Page firm since the V/1500, and it is not

First pilot's controls and instruments. The second pilot sits on the starboard side and can supervise the instruments mounted on that end of the panel.

without interest to note that the wing span is the same as that of the O/400 of 1915, and the two wing areas also the same within a little. But whereas the O/400 had a loaded weight of 14,000 lb., the Halifax at full load weighs something like 60,000 lb. Apart from the change to all-metal construction which has taken place, it is this increase in wing loading which has made the Halifax and Short Stirling bombers possible; and it is fair to say that in making this high wing loading possible the Handley Page Company has taken a prominent part. The lift slot and the slotted flap were products of this company, and although the former is not used on the Halifax, the research and development work carried out in connection with it have borne fruit in directions which have benefited design as a whole. Even with such aids to high wing loadings, the heavy bomber of to-day would not have been feasible but for the vast improvement in flying technique and piloting skill which has grown up since the days of the O/400.

The Halifax, at full speed, flies with its tail slightly up, as the wings are set at a fairly large angle on the fuselage so as to obtain the necessary ground angle without the need for a very stilty undercarriage.

In examining the Handley Page Halifax down to the minutest detail, as we have been privileged to do, thanks to the courtesy of the Handley Page Company and the Ministry of Aircraft Production, two things in particular impress us; they appear contradictory but are not so in fact. One is that the tremendous task of first producing thousands of drawings and scores of jigs, without which the aircraft could not be produced at all, has been possible, so that actual production can be, and is, on quite a large scale. The other is that, for an aircraft which has to carry the complexity of equipment which an inspection of the Halifax discloses, the primary structure is remarkably simple. The only complication in the machine is that which is due to the nature of the equipment. No compli-

cation is caused by the structure having to carry its stresses as such.

The function of the Halifax being to carry the greatest possible bomb load the longest possible distance, with sufficient speed to get to distant targets during the darkness of night, the general characteristics were determined by the fact that no aircraft engine was available, two units of which would lift the desired load at the necessary speed. The machine had, therefore, perforce to be a four-engined type. That introduced complication number one. Not only had engine instruments and controls to be quadrupled, but the fuel system became more involved owing to the fact that any and all engines had to be capable of being fed from any and all tanks, and a greater quantity of fuel had to

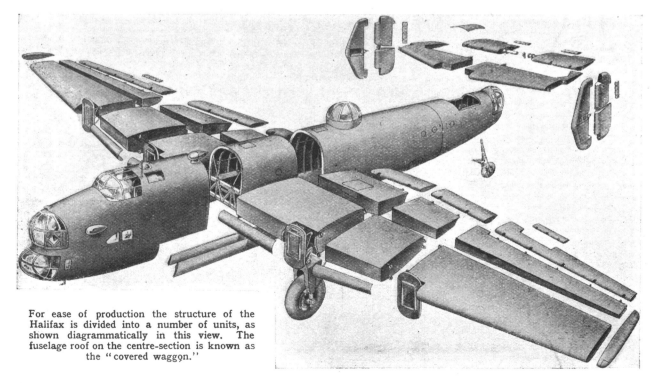

For ease of production the structure of the Halifax is divided into a number of units, as shown diagrammatically in this view. The fuselage roof on the centre-section is known as the "covered waggon."

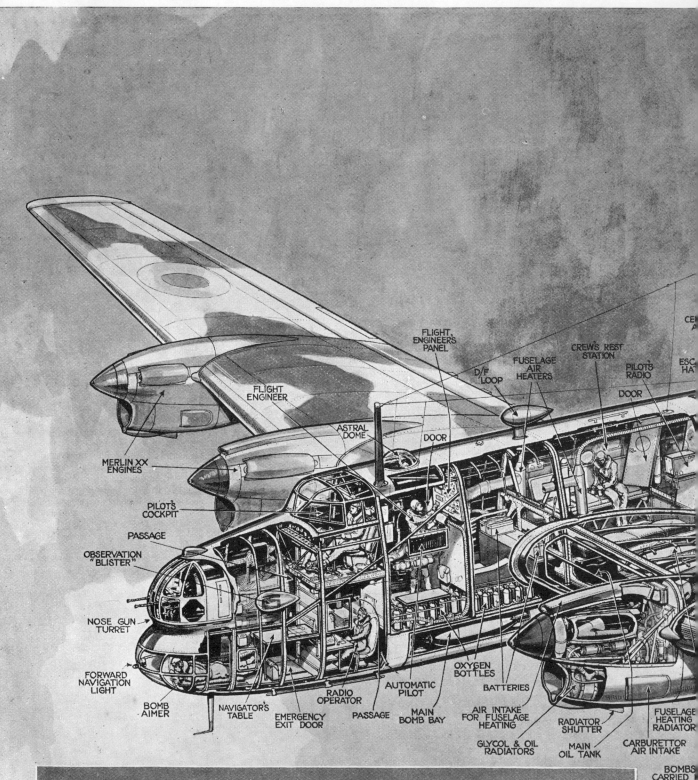

FLIGHT, ENGINEERS PANEL

CREWS REST STATION

D/F LOOP

FUSELAGE AIR HEATERS

PILOTS RADIO

FLIGHT ENGINEER

DOOR

ASTRAL DOME

DOOR

MERLIN XX ENGINES

PILOT'S COCKPIT

PASSAGE

OBSERVATION "BLISTER"

NOSE GUN TURRET

FORWARD NAVIGATION LIGHT

BOMB AIMER

NAVIGATOR'S TABLE

EMERGENCY EXIT DOOR

RADIO OPERATOR

AUTOMATIC PILOT

PASSAGE

MAIN BOMB BAY

OXYGEN BOTTLES

BATTERIES

AIR INTAKE FOR FUSELAGE HEATING

GLYCOL & OIL RADIATORS

RADIATOR SHUTTER

MAIN OIL TANK

FUSELAGE HEATING RADIATOR

CARBURETTOR AIR INTAKE

BOMBS CARRIED

DIMENSIONS

Wing span : 99ft.   Height : 22ft.
Wing area : 1,250 sq. ft.   Fuselage height : 9ft. 6in.
Length o.a. : 70ft.   Fuselage width : 5ft. 6in.

ARMAMENT

Two Browning .303 machine guns in nose turret
Two Browning .303 machine guns in dorsal turret
Four Browning .303 machine guns in tail turret

WEIGHT AND PERFORMANCE

Loaded weight : 60,000 lb.   Range (max.) : 3,000 miles approx.
Maximum speed : 300 m.p.h. approx.   Maximum bomb load : $5\frac{1}{2}$ tons

ENGINES

Four Rolls-Royce Merlin (1,175 h.p. each at 20,500ft.)

CREW

Seven : Two pilots ; navigator/bomb-aimer ; W/T operator ;
front gunner ; midship gunner ; tail gunner

REAR TURRET
AUXILIARY
AMMUNITION

DOOR

MASTER
COMPASS
GYRO

LAVATORY

AUXILIARY
AMMUNITION
CHUTES

MAIN
DOOR

FLARE
CHUTE

RECONNAISSANCE
FLARES

STOWED
DINGHY

MAIN PETROL
TANKS

PETROL
JETTISONING
OUTLETS

TWIN LANDING
LIGHTS

FLIGHT
COPYRIGHT

MAX MILLAR

be carried so as to supply the extra power.

Then came the question of bomb load. Had it merely been desired to carry one very large bomb in a bay in the fuselage, the matter would have been simple. The concentrated load would have been large, but there would have been no difficulty in providing for that. It is, however, not on every raid that a single or even two very large bombs will be the most suitable cargo. There are times when a larger number of smaller bombs are more appropriate to the target ; and so provision had to be made for stowing some bombs in the wings and some in the bomb bay in the floor of the fuselage. They could, presumably, have been worked into the design by making the bomb bay very long, but that would have introduced difficulties with the centre of gravity, which would have moved so far in a fore and aft direction that serious instability might well have arisen unless front and rear bombs were dropped

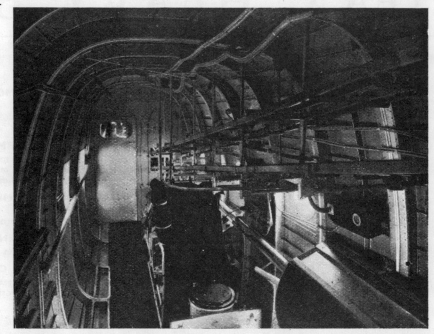

View in the rear compartment looking aft and showing ammunition rails. The door in the background leads to the tail gunner's compartment.

simultaneously, a procedure which might not always be desirable.

Considerations such as those outlined led to the Halifax becoming what it is, a four-engined cantilever monoplane, with the wing set approximately half-way up the sides of the fuselage. Defensive armament had to be provided in nose and tail, as well as on top of the fuselage, although we have never quite understood why a nose turret should be needed in a heavy night bomber, which is not likely to attack any hostile aircraft except fighters, and they are not likely to attack from in front.

General Design

With such questions as number of engines, load of bombs and number of gun turrets settled beforehand, the general design could be begun, and the outline sketched out. The proportions of the Halifax are so good that the great size of the aircraft does not obtrude itself on the onlooker. It looks large, certainly, but does not convey an impression of 27 tons hurtling through the air at 300 m.p.h. or so. We imagine that Mr. Volkert,

Handley Page's chief designer, made good use of his project engineer, Mr. Haines, in deciding upon the lines of the machine, which are uncommonly good. It is not very difficult to make a small aircraft pretty, but it is very easy to make a large one look ugly. That has been avoided in the Halifax, which is easily the best-looking machine that firm has produced. The nose and tail gun turrets have been worked into the lines in a way that is very pleasing, and only the dorsal turret mars the continuity ; that, however, was unavoidable. A "dustbin" underneath would be even worse as an eyesore.

The surface of the Halifax is perfectly smooth when the fuselage and wings leave their jigs, as flush-riveting is employed. But that aid to laminar flow does not last

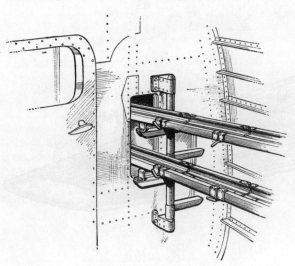

Rails carry ammunition to the tail gunner. Here they are shown at the point where they pass through the bulkhead of the tail compartment.

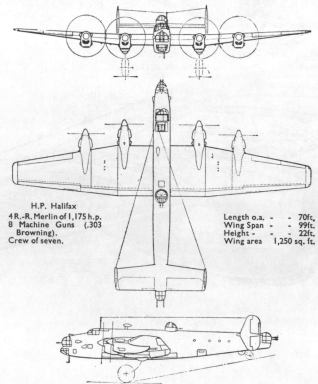

H.P. Halifax
4 R.-R. Merlin of 1,175 h.p.
8 Machine Guns (.303 Browning).
Crew of seven.

Length o.a. - - 70ft.
Wing Span - - 99ft.
Height - - 22ft.
Wing area 1,250 sq. ft.

very long; in fact, it never sees the light of day, for in the dope shop is applied, on all under surfaces, that most black and most matt of all paints, the night-bomber black which reflects practically no light from the searchlights, but which must reduce the speed quite as much as would ordinary round-headed rivets.

Inside the fuselage the space is divided into a number of compartments for the various members of the crew. In the extreme nose is the position for the prone bomb-aimer, and as he is also the navigator his folding chart table, instruments, etc., are in the same compartment, a little farther aft. Above him, on the top floor, is the front gunner's turret, with two Browning .303 machine guns and their ammunition. Separated from the navigator's compartment by a partition which runs half-way across the width of the fuselage is the wireless operator's cabin, and above that the pilot's cockpit. Then follows the compartment for the flight engineer, who supervises a number of indicators. He has a folding seat and sits with his back to the second pilot on the starboard side of the cabin. The flight engineer's compartment is closed at the back by an armour plate bulkhead and door. Then follows a large compartment, which extends from the flight engineer's bulkhead to the rear wing spar, above which is a wooden bulkhead, which is really more of a

draught screen than anything else, and aft of that is a large stowage space in which a swinging ladder gives access to the dorsal gun turret. This turret has two Browning .303 machine guns.

Aft of the turret is a w.c. screened off by a black curtain, and a drop in floor level affords head room to walk right

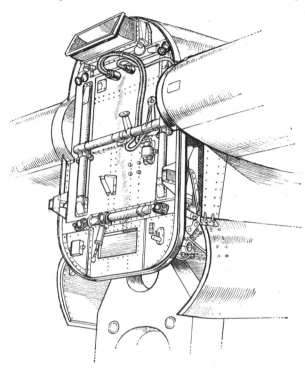

The bulkheads of the inboard engines are mounted at the ends of the wing centre section. The intermediate wing portion is shown in place in this view, as is also the undercarriage. The four pick-up points for the engine-bearers are shown. They are in the form of ball and socket joints. The radiator at the top heats the air used for warming the crew's stations.

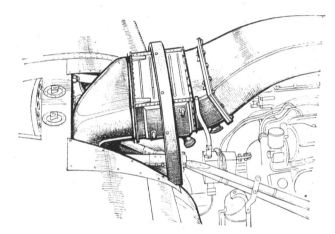

The radiator on the port inboard engine bulkhead supplies hot air through a large pipe to the crew's stations inside the fuselage.

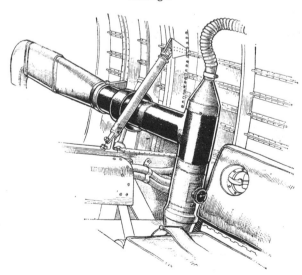

Heating air for the crew's stations is taken from a special radiator in one of the engine nacelles. Smaller branch pipes lead to different parts of the fuselage so as to heat the whole. The handle in the recess operates the undercarriage "up" lock if the hydraulic system should fail.

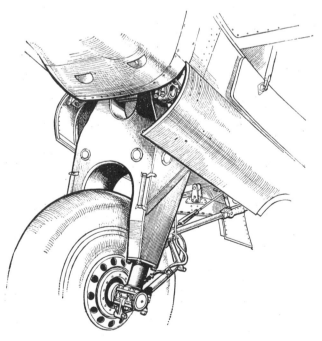

The Messier undercarriage of the Halifax carries Dunlop wheels fitted with pneumatic brakes. The wheel fork is a huge light-alloy casting.

up to the sheet-metal partition which separates the fuselage from the tail wheel compartment and tail gun turret. The latter is a real sting in the tail, mounting four .303 Brownings, which must compensate "tail-end Charlie" quite a lot for his somewhat lonesome post and separation from the rest of the crew.

The bomb bay is, of course, located under the fuselage floor. Having seen the general layout, which in the main shows the gangway and clear space on the starboard side, the equipment on the port, it may be of interest to go back and examine in more detail some of the equipment and its location.

Lightening the Pilot's Task

By carrying a crew of seven it has been possible to relieve the pilot of some of the indicators; in fact, the flight engineer and second pilot attend to all except those which are essential to the actual piloting of the aircraft. The first pilot sits on the port side, with a control wheel of the "spectacle" type in front of him. Inside the spectacles are a second, smaller pair. These work the wheel brakes. At a higher level, and running right across to the starboard side of the fuselage, above the entrance to the navigator/bomb-aimer's compartment, is the main instrument panel. Set into it, close to the port side of the compartment, is a smaller panel spring-mounted. This carries the following dials: airspeed indicator; artificial horizon; rate of climb indicator; altimeter; direction indicator; and turn indicator. Carried on a separate small panel close to the wall of the fuselage are a C.S. bombsight steering indicator and, below it, a blind-landing indicator.

Below the main vertical panel is a small sloping panel

The crew's rest station has upholstered settees along the sides. The large tubes on the right are the hot-air leads. Branches run to different parts of the fuselage.

strip carrying oxygen flow meter; auto-control pressure indicator; air temperature gauge; repeater compass (the master gyro compass is mounted in the rear fuselage compartment); wing flap indicator; four boost gauges and four double main engine switches; the undercarriage indicators and the bomb firing switch. These dials are all under the eyes of the first pilot—and quite enough, one would say —but only a fraction of what he would have to survey if a flight engineer were not carried.

The starboard half, or so, of the main vertical panel carries dials which can be observed by the second pilot when he is seated in his sliding seat near the starboard wall of the compartment. The instruments mounted here are: four engine rev indicators; vacuum pump change-over cock; bomb door warning lights; the bomb jettison handle; an altimeter; oxygen supply indicator; wheel brake pressure gauge; and fuel jettison valve.

Engine Controls

Reverting to the equipment for the first pilot, there is a control pedestal approximately in the centre of the compartment which carries at the top the four throttle levers side by side. Below these are, also side by side, the four levers which control the four Rotol airscrews, and below them are the cut-out lever of the automatic boost control, the mixture lever, and the control lever which selects the blower speed. In the "down" position this lever provides medium boost, and in the "up" position full supercharge.

Mention has been made above of the electric repeater compass. In addition, there is a normal magnetic compass, mounted under the instrument board and in front of the joy stick.

Even this list does not exhaust the equipment in the first pilot's compartment. On the port wall are the switches for "cutting-in" and "cutting-out" the automatic pilot, and the radio tuning controls. Next to the first pilot's seat, on his right, are the levers for operating the hydraulic services such as bomb doors, flaps and undercarriage. Placed in that particular position, they are within reach of, and can, if necessary, be worked by, the second pilot. On the "ground floor," below the pilots, is the radio

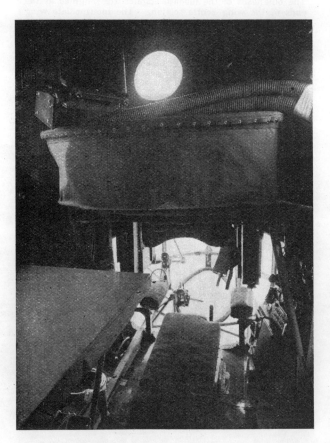

The prone bomber's station in the nose. Above it on the left is the navigator's table. The circular window at the top is just behind the nose gun turret.

operator's compartment. Here, of course, is installed all the wireless equipment, with the exception of the loop aerial, which is mounted on top of the fuselage farther aft, and is distantly controlled. Of the transmitting and receiving equipment it is, perhaps, better to say nothing. It may or may not be known to the enemy, and there is little point in taking a chance on giving him information. At any rate, our radio equipment is, by common consent, better than the German.

Navigating in Comfort

The navigator's compartment is comparatively comfortably furnished, with a quite large folding chart table at which he can plot his courses and generally work in comfort. The type of parallel-motion equipment familiar from the aircraft draughtsman's board is used in place of the parallel rulers of the sea navigator, and the table is illuminated by a small Terry Anglepoise lamp. In addition to his own outfit, the navigator is also provided with an altimeter, air temperature gauge, and an airspeed indicator.

Proceeding aft, we come to the flight engineer's compartment, which is uncommonly well stocked with dials. Four engines need a lot of surveillance, and the fact that they are out in the wings means that they are out of sight and their well-being can only be ascertained by distantly placed dials. Most of the flight engineer's dials are placed on the after wall of the compartment, which is, as previously mentioned, of armour plate, so that the delicate instruments, as well as the forward crew, are protected against attack from behind. On this wall of the flight engineer's compartment are found fuel tank content gauges (quite an excellent array of them), oil temperature and oil pressure gauges, radiator flap controls, and airscrew anti-icer controls.

Passing aft through the door in the armour-plate bulkhead, we come to a compartment partly used for stowage of all manner of equipment, and partly as a rest station for members of the crew. Between the front and rear wing spars upholstered seats run along both outer walls. The main fuel tank cocks are housed under the seats, and there are also catches for releasing the undercarriages from their "up" position, should the hydraulic system fail. A hand-operated pump is provided, so that in the event of the power supply going wrong the undercarriages can be raised and lowered by man-power. At the forward end of this compartment is the accumulator for the hydraulic system which operates the bomb doors; there also are some of the oxygen bottles which supply the 13 points in the

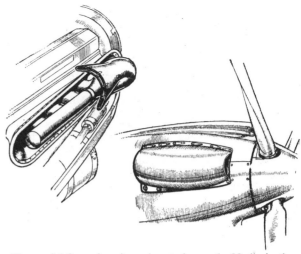

The special flame damping exhaust pipe on the Merlin in the Halifax is shown on the left. An outer cowling (right) obscures the exhaust flames still more. There is thus little to give away the position of the machine to the night fighters.

fuselage from which the members of the crew obtain their oxygen by plugging into bayonet sockets.

The rear end of this compartment is closed by a plywood draught wall, aft of which is a large stowage space for such items as flares, etc. A swinging ladder gives access to the dorsal two-gun turret, which, like those in nose and stern, is of Boulton-Paul design and manufacture. Aft of the ladder are racks for sea markers and ammunition, and here also start the conveyor rails along which ammunition is supplied to the tail gunner.

Aft of here there is a drop in floor level, the floor being directly on the bottom of the fuselage. At this point, on the port side, there is the small door through which the crew enter the machine. Also, as mentioned above, the w.c. is located here, on the port side, and aft of that, elaborately swung in gimbals and isolated from vibration, is the master gyro compass; repeater compasses are located in the pilot's and navigator's compartments.

The compartment in the rear end of the fuselage houses a large dome for the retractable tailwheel, and at its rear end gives access to the gun turret in the stern.

The Heating System

That completes our survey of the interior of the Halifax. It should, however, be mentioned that, in addition to the oxygen supply, the comfort of the crew is looked after by a very effective system of heating. The hot air is not, as is usually the case, obtained from muffs around one or more exhaust pipes. Instead there are two special radiators incorporated in the glycol cooling system, one behind and above each of the inboard engines. Air, under control, enters the engine nacelles and is passed through these radiators, where it is heated during its passage, and is then led through flexible tubes of large diameter to the interior of the fuselage. Inside the fuselage the large-diameter pipes branch into smaller pipes, which run to the different compartments.

It might also be mentioned that the flying controls are of the Saunders type described in *Flight* of January 1st, 1942. This type of control serves a dual purpose, since a sliding motion is used for the main controls, such as rudders and elevators, while a rotary motion of the same tubes operates lighter controls, such as tabs.

Housed in the wings is, next to the fuselage, a bomb compartment on each side, and outboard of them are the fuel

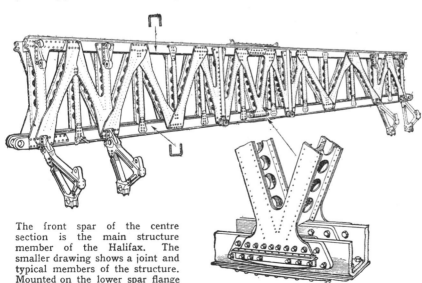

The front spar of the centre section is the main structure member of the Halifax. The smaller drawing shows a joint and typical members of the structure. Mounted on the lower spar flange are the undercarriage supports.

tanks. Some are placed between the main wing spars, and others in the leading-edge in front of the front spar. All tanks are, of course, leak-proofed with rubber. The placing of the tanks is well shown on Mr. Millar's drawing on pp. 398a and b. Provision is made for jettisoning the fuel in emergency. The pipes (see sketch opposite) lead to the trailing-edge, and a sleeve of rubber on each pipe permits the end of the nozzle to move up and down with the wing flap. The pipes are fairly large and consequently detract somewhat from the appearance of the machine, but that is unavoidable in view of the quantity of fuel that may have to be jettisoned.

Tapering Wings

In plan view the wing shows a fairly pronounced taper, the actual wing chords being 16ft. at the root and 6ft.-6in. at the tip.

The four Rolls-Royce Merlin XX engines are mounted ahead of the leading-edge, the two inboard engines being slightly ahead of the two outboard, so that the airscrews of adjacent engines are not in the same plane.

An interesting point about the engine installation is that great care has been taken over the flame damping of the exhaust. The special exhaust pipes in themselves reduce the amount of visible flame, and the rest is hidden by an exhaust cowl placed over the exhaust pipe.

Mounted on the port inboard engine is a Heywood compressor for the pneumatic brake system, and each of the inboard engines drives a 24-volt 1,000-watt electric generator, that on the port engine supplying the lighting system, while the generator on the starboard engine furnishes power for engine-starting, feathering of the Rotol airscrews, etc.

Messier undercarriages carry Dunlop wheels measuring 24in. by 19in. Retraction into the engine nacelles is by the usual "broken" rear strut. Normally the undercarriages are operated by hydraulic power, but a hand pump in the fuselage forms an auxiliary means of operation.

Should the entire hydraulic system fail, through enemy action, for example, pieces of stretched rubber cord assist

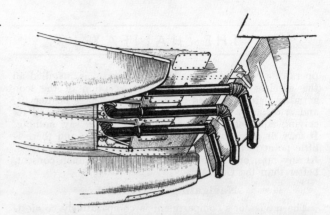

Jettison pipe on the Halifax carrying fuel clear of the trailing-edge. To allow the wing flap to deflect a flexible rubber sleeve is used.

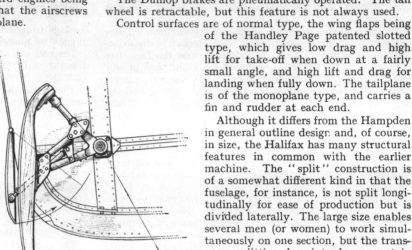

The very ingenious bomb doors of the Halifax are shown here in the "up" position. When the doors are closed the two portions lie edge to edge.

the operation. Some idea of the size of the Halifax may be formed from the fact that the wheel track is 24ft. 8in.

The Dunlop brakes are pneumatically operated. The tail wheel is retractable, but this feature is not always used.

Control surfaces are of normal type, the wing flaps being of the Handley Page patented slotted type, which gives low drag and high lift for take-off when down at a fairly small angle, and high lift and drag for landing when fully down. The tailplane is of the monoplane type, and carries a fin and rudder at each end.

Although it differs from the Hampden in general outline design and, of course, in size, the Halifax has many structural features in common with the earlier machine. The "split" construction is of a somewhat different kind in that the fuselage, for instance, is not split longitudinally for ease of production but is divided laterally. The large size enables several men (or women) to work simultaneously on one section, but the transverse splitting does introduce a certain amount of complication in that electric and hydraulic leads have to be "cut" at the fuselage joints. This means that quick connectors have to be used. In the case of the electric leads this is accomplished by adopting the Breeze system of wiring, with multi-pin connectors.

In the rear portion of the fuselage, where the stresses are not so great, the joints between fuselage portions are of very simple type. The end ring or frame of each portion is reinforced by and riveted to a stiffening ring of extruded L-section. The longer limb of the L, which tapers towards its free edge, is riveted to the skin, while the shorter limb, which is a good deal thicker, is riveted to the normal frame, and also has holes in it for the numerous small bolts by which it is attached to the corresponding ring of the next fuselage section. Where greater stresses are encountered, such as, for example, where the fuselage bomb bay is attached to the floor, special forgings are used to reinforce the connection.

The normal main frames of the fuselage are of built-up box section, with the flanges turned outwards for ease of riveting, and with an internal channel section for stiffening. The intermediate frames are of Z-section, formed from sheet. The frames are notched for the stringers, which are of "figure-two" section.

In the structure of the wing, the front spar of the centre-section forms the backbone. It is a veritable bridge girder, with very thick extruded channel sections for flanges, and vertical and diagonal struts for tie members. These latter are of a form generally similar to the fuselage frames (that is to say, box-sections with outwardly

The Handley Page Gyral bomb winch. This can be placed on the wing or in the fuselage, the bomb weight being taken by the swivel, and the "feet" merely steady the winch.

This three-quarter rear view of the Halifax shows an earlier production and was taken before a dorsal gun turret was fitted.

turned flanges), but the material of the boxes, especially the flat front and rear plates, is many times thicker, as the loads in this neighbourhood are very large. The general construction of the centre-section front spar is shown by a sketch.

The centre-section rear spar is of different construction, with extruded T-section flanges and solid sheet web. A similar construction is employed for both front and rear spars in the outer wing portions, but the flange sections change from T to L. The wing ribs in the centre-section carry heavy loads and have solid sheet webs riveted between two L-section flanges placed back to back.

The rib webs are stiffened by vertical channel sections, one on each side of the web for the main stiffeners and on channel on one side for the intermediate stiffeners.

The trailing-edge ribs are of slightly different construction. The main ribs have channel-section flanges placed with the open side towards the skin. Instead of the solid sheet web of the between spar ribs, the top and bottom channels are connected by diagonal tubes, attached to the flange channel sides by fishplates. The spanwise stringers of the wing skin are cut at their intersection with the rib flanges.

The sting in the tail. The gunner's turret with its four Browning machine guns.

Unit Construction

In the construction of the wing, as in that of the fuselage, small assemblies are formed into larger ones, and finally into quite large units, so that the work of assembly permits the greatest possible number of workers to be employed simultaneously. The actual production methods in force in the Handley Page works, which are very interesting, will be dealt with in detail in our associated journal *Aircraft Production.*

An ingenious system has been evolved for transporting the large wing and fuselage portions from the manufacturing to the assembly shops, which are situated elsewhere. The wing centre-section, for example, is transported in a vertical position, with the engine mountings and bulkheads already in place, and the fuselage top (known as " the covered wagon ") already attached.

The general construction and internal layout are shown in the large drawing by Mr. M. A. Millar on page **14**

and **15**. The system of breaking down the structure into a number of units is illustrated diagrammatically on page **15**. The main dimensions of the Halifax are: Wing span 99ft.; wing area 1,250 sq. ft.; length o.a. 70ft. 1in.; fuselage width (max.) 5ft. 6in.; fuselage height (max.) 9ft. 6in. Detailed performance figures may not be given, but the maximum speed is in the neighbourhood of 300 m.p.h. Maximum range is about 3,000 miles, and maximum bomb load 5½ tons. The two do not, of course, occur simultaneously.

The four Rolls-Royce Merlin XX engines develop 1,175 h.p. each, at 20,500ft., and drive Rotol three-bladed, fully feathering airscrews of 12ft. 6in. diameter.

Take-off and landing characteristics are very good, in spite of a wing loading of 47 lb./sq. ft.

Readers who would like to compare the Halifax with the Short Stirling heavy bomber are referred to our issue of January 29th, 1942, in which we published a long illustrated description of that machine.

IX—THE HANDLEY PAGE HALIFAX

THOSE who believe that breeding tells will readily place the Halifax in the front rank of heavy bombers. No other aeroplane now in service with Bomber Command has a longer pedigree or a more famous ancestry. It is the youngest member of a long line of aeroplanes which began with the Handley Page 0/100 of 1915 and includes many other notable military types and several which distinguished themselves in civil and commercial flying.

Big bombers and civil transports as they exist to-day owe a great deal to Handley Page Ltd. When Mr. F. Handley Page founded his company in 1910 he started an organisation which within five years had evolved the first practical heavy bomber and within ten had put into service the first multi-engined air-liners in the World. Inspired by such a weighty start in life the Company has ever since pursued a most energetic policy in developing the large aeroplane. Thus, some 30 years of experience in design, construction and operation are incorporated in the latest Handley Page bomber.

The design of the Halifax originated in a two-motor design to the Air Ministry medium bomber specification P.13/36 of 1936. Later this aeroplane—the H.P.56—was altered to take four Merlins instead of two Vultures as originally planned and became known as the H.P.57— later the Halifax. In this form it first flew on October 25, 1939. The Halifax I, with two Boulton Paul turrets and four 1,145 h.p. Rolls-Royce Merlin X motors was by then already in large-scale production and it started to go into service in November, 1940.

After the first production batch had been completed the Halifax II with the 1,280 h.p. Rolls-Royce Merlin XX motors superseded the original version. The first machines of the new series had the same armament as the Halifax I, but more recent examples have an additional Boulton Paul turret on top of the fuselage.

The Halifax first went into action on March 11, 1941, against targets at Le Havre, and ever since it has been used in steadily increasing numbers by night, and (less frequently) by day.

Perhaps the most spectacular of daylight operations by the Halifax was the famous attack on the Scharnhorst at La Pallice on July 24, 1941. On that day, an unescorted force of these bombers attacked the German battle-cruiser which had just slipped out of Brest. Two hits were made on the warship which then returned to Brest where it remained until the carefully planned and elaborately executed escape of the imprisoned warships enabled them to regain their home ports in a battered condition. During operations at La Pallice some of the Halifaxes were subjected to fierce and persistent attacks by fighters and the manner in which these were beaten off by the turret-mounted guns was the clearest proof up to that time of the effectiveness of the power-operated gun turret.

The tail turret in the Halifax is remarkably compact, yet mounts four Brownings with servo-feed, and is unusually comfortable for the gunner. The comfort of the tail gunner on long flights has a direct bearing on his efficiency and, therefore, on the safety of the bomber as a whole.

On night work the Halifax has played a constantly important part in the R.A.F.'s mounting offensive. By the end of 1941 most of the important European targets so far visited by the R.A.F. had received its unwelcome attention. More recently it has taken part in the devastating attacks on the German Baltic ports of Lübeck, Rostock and Warnemünde.

Although the many Handley Page aeroplanes of the past have included some famous bombers there have also been some equally historic civil types. These did much as pioneers of commercial aviation in the years between the two World Wars. The Company while busily engaged on commercial types always maintained a close interest in bomber development even in the lean "disarmament" years when little official support was forthcoming. This was fortunate for the Nation; when War came Handley Page bombers, as efficient as ever, formed a vital part of our bombing force. They will continue to do so until the end of the War. When peace is restored Handley Page will be able to turn again to the needs of air transport, and play a leading part in designing and building the aeroplanes that will help to make Britain pre-eminent in air commerce.

HALIFAX

THERE are men living in this country to-day who were deprived ("deprived" is the right word) of the chance to bomb Berlin in the last war by the sudden surrender of the Kaiser's army in November, 1918. Those men would have set out on their great adventure in Handley Page V/1500 bombers. These machines, the biggest anyone had seen at that time, were four-engined aircraft, and special bombs weighing 3,500 lb. had been designed for "special delivery" to the enemy's unscathed capital. At the eleventh hour the raid was cancelled.

It is rather in the nature of just compensation, therefore, that Handley Page should provide, during this war, another four-engined bomber which is every bit as modern as were those old biplanes of more than 20 years ago, with the difference that, this time, they are getting plenty of chances to hit the Hun where it hurts him most, namely, in his own country. The Halifax is proving itself to be one of our most successful long-range bombers, having a maximum bomb load of 5½ tons, a maximum range of about 3,000 miles, and a top speed of approximately 300 m.p.h. These maximum figures, of course, are not all obtained simultaneously.

Of the mid-wing type, with twin fins and rudders, the Halifax is of all-metal construction with smooth, stressed-skin covering except for the control surfaces which are fabric covered. The fuselage, which is "slab-sided" in section, is of sufficient depth to enable the crew to move about in an upright position, but in spite of its comparative roominess it gives no impression of clumsy bulk, thanks to its well-proportioned lines. Incidentally, the fuselage is constructed in jig-built sections which is the usual Handley Page practice and which greatly facilitates rapid production.

Power is supplied by four Rolls-Royce Merlin XX liquid-cooled, V-shaped 12-cylinder engines, each giving 1,175 h.p. at 20,500ft., and fitted with Rotol three-bladed fully feathering c.s. airscrews. Flame-damping ejector exhausts are employed.

The armament of the Halifax comprises two Boulton-Paul electrically operated two-gun turrets, one in the nose and one amidships above the trailing-edge of the wings, and a four-gun Boulton-Paul turret in the extreme tail of the fuselage.

Fitted with de-icing equipment and with oxygen apparatus for its crew of seven, the Halifax is described by its pilots as easy to fly and very manœuvrable.

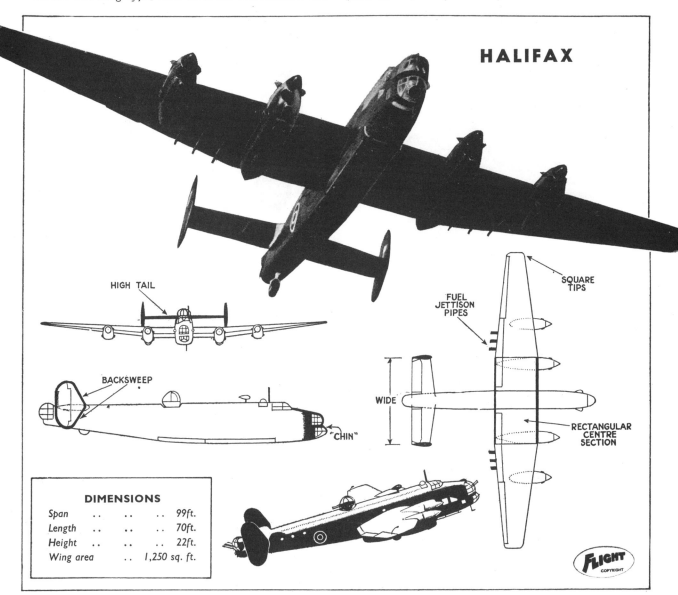

HALIFAX

HIGH TAIL

SQUARE TIPS

FUEL JETTISON PIPES

BACKSWEEP

WIDE

"CHIN"

RECTANGULAR CENTRE SECTION

DIMENSIONS

Span	..	..	.. 99ft.
Length	..	..	.. 70ft.
Height	..	..	.. 22ft.
Wing area		..	1,250 sq. ft.

FLIGHT COPYRIGHT

HANDLEY PAGE HALIFAX

Some Detail Sketches, and a New Set of Striking Photographs by Our Chief Photographer of a Halifax Being Put Through Its Paces by Flt. Lt. J. R. Talbot, Handley Page's Chief Test Pilot

The above photograph of a Halifax in formation with the photographer's aircraft shows how manoeuvrable it is despite its 27 tons all-up weight. Of interest also in this picture are the asbestos muffs over the exhaust ports which damp the exhaust flames while flying at night and make it more difficult for the enemy night fighters to spot the machine.

(Above) As the Halifax turns away the dead-black paint of the underside puts the machine in silhouette. The three projections behind the trailing edge of each wing are the pipes used to jettison fuel in case of emergency.

(Right) A three-quarter rear view which emphasises the excellent field of fire covered by the three power-operated gun turrets. For all its 99ft. span the Halifax is a graceful machine and appears smaller than it actually is.

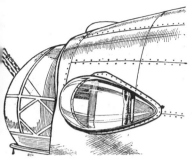

The two-gun turret and streamlined see - behind blister in the nose.

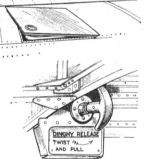

Two sketches showing how the inflatable dinghy is stowed in the wing and the method of release.

DINGHY RELEASE
TWIST
AND PULL

(Above) The Handley Page Halifax has not only proved itself a formidable bomber, but also has earned itself an enviable reputation for shooting down enemy fighters.

(Right) Oxygen-bottle storage in the floor behind the pilot.

(Below) A study of a Halifax as seen from beneath the tail of a sister aircraft.

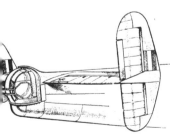

A sketch of the tail-plane with its "end-plate" fins and rudders. The rear turret has a traverse of 180 degrees.

"HALIFAX"

'The Aeroplane' photograph

LUBECK

ROSTOCK

WARNEMUNDE

COLOGNE

ESSEN

BREMEN

HANDLEY-PAGE LIMITED LONDON

THE HANDLEY PAGE HALIFAX II

(Four Rolls-Royce Merlin XX motors)

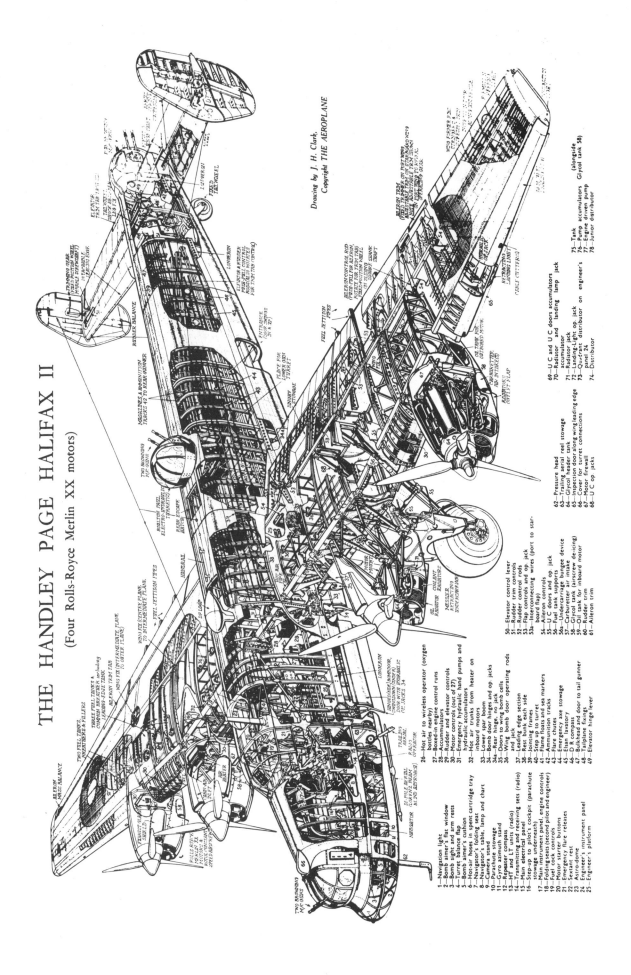

Drawing by J. H. Clark.
Copyright THE AEROPLANE

1—Navigation light
2—Bomb aimer's flat window
3—Bomb sight and arm rests
4—Turret balance
5—Bomb aimer's cushion
6—Hot-air hoses in spent cartridge tray
7—Navigator's folding seat
8—Navigator's table, lamp and chart
9—Camera stand
10—Parachute stowage
11—Gyro azimuth stand
12—Repeater compass
13—HT and LT units (radio)
14—Transmitting and receiving sets (radio)
15—Main electrical panel
16—Step-up to pilot's cockpit (parachute stowage underneath)
17—Main instrument panel, engine controls
18—Folding seats (second pilot and engineer)
19—Fuel cock controls
20—Motor starter buttons
21—Emergency flare releases
22—Sextant rest
23—D R compass
24—Engineer's instrument panel
25—Engineer's platform
26—Hot air to wireless operator (oxygen bottles nearby)
27—Boxed-in engine control runs
28—Accumulators
29—Rudder and elevator controls
30—Motor controls (out of 27)
31—Emergency hydraulic hand pumps and jack
32—Hot-air trunks from heater on inboard motors
33—Lower spar boom
34—Bomb door hinges and op jacks
34a—Rear hinge, no jack
35—Doors to wing bomb cells
36—Wing bomb door operating rods and jack
37—Leading edge section
38—Rest bunk each side
39—Jointing frames
40—Step up to turret
41—Flame floats and sea markers
42—Ammunition tracks
43—Flare chutes
44—Emergency axe stowage
45—Elsan lavatory
46—D R compass
47—Bulkhead and door to tail gunner
48—Tailplane fixing
49—Elevator hinge lever
50—Elevator control lever
51—Rudder trim controls
52—Rudder control rods
53—Flap controls and op jack
53a—Interconnecting wires (port to starboard flap)
54—Aileron controls
55—U C doors and op jack
56—Fuel tank supports
56a—Undercarriage bungee device
57—Carburetter air intake
58—Glycol header tank
59—Oil tank for inboard motor
60—Rudder trim
61—Aileron trim
62—Pressure head
63—Trailing aerial reel stowage
64—Glycol header tank
65—Inspection door along wing leading edge
66—Cover for turret connections
67—Motor firewall
68—U C op jacks
69—U C and U C doors accumulators
70—Radiator and landing lamp jack
71—Radiator jack
72—Landing-light op. jack
73—Quadrant distributor on engineer's panel 24
74—Distributor
75—Tank
76—Pump accumulators (alongside Glycol tank 58)
77—Engine driven pump
78—Junior distributor

27

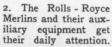

2. The Rolls - Royce Merlins and their auxiliary equipment get their daily attention.

3. A spinner is removed to attend to the Rotol airscrew.

1. A Handley Page Halifax at its dispersal point, overhauled and ready for the night's operations.

MAINTAINING our air offensive over Germany is so frequently thought of only in terms of aircraft output and replacement, that the problems of servicing and overhauling—or, in other words, keeping machines operationally airworthy—is often forgotten To illustrate these points we have selected a Halifax, not because that type is any more complicated than any other four-engined heavy bomber but because it is representative of its type.

In the 1914-18 war the proportion of aircraft on charge to personnel employed was 22,171 to 291,152. They were very simple types by comparison with the complicated structures which now take their loads of five, six or seven tons of bombs to Germany, and when one remembers all the people employed, apart from the uniformed personnel actually handling the aircraft, the numbers must to-day amount to many thousands per machine. There are, for instance, those who dig the metal from the earth and those who smelt it. There are those who bring material from across the globe in ships

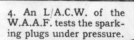

4. An L/A.C.W. of the W.A.A.F. tests the sparking plugs under pressure.

5. All the multiplicity of instruments receive a daily inspection and check for function and accuracy.

6. "George," the automatic pilot, is adjusted by a highly skilled instrument repairer. This picture also shows a little of the complicated electric wiring and "plumbing" of modern aircraft.

TAKES OFF

and the employees of the aircraft industry who fabricate the aircraft. Each operational bomber must also be debited with its share of training aircraft and training personnel. Hospital staffs, records, transport, equipment and finance all contribute their quota. Finally, all these people, whose whole time is employed in producing aircraft, have to be fed, clothed and housed. When all this is considered, it makes one realise how far the country has marched from the single-figure bomber raids of 1940 to the four-figure raids of 1942.

7. Inter-com. is of vital importance and must be free from crackles and bangs.

8. Radio must be 100 per cent. right because on this may depend the lives of the whole crew.

9. The navigator himself checks the compasses in the Halifax with the aid of an external instrument.

10. Oxygen bottles have to be filled to ensure a plentiful supply at altitude.

11. A supply of compressed air is necessary.

12. Hundreds of gallons of high grade fuel is pumped aboard.

13. Making belts of small arms ammunition by machine. The links are in the tall upright container and the rounds are fed into the hopper.

BEFORE A BOMBER TAKES OFF

To what size these raids may grow before Germany throws up the sponge can only be a matter for conjecture. But it is not difficult to foresee the time when the Americans and ourselves, working in double harness, will be able to find 2,000 bombers to raid any target in the Reich.

15. After the disintegrating belts have been made, they are passed through an aligning machine to ensure, as far as possible, that there shall be no stoppages from this cause.

14. On the armourer's bench the Browning guns are stripped, cleaned and re-erected

16. Guns are replaced in the power-operated turrets and the working of the turret checked.

17. From a bomb depot come huge trailers loaded with boxes of incendiary bombs of different weights.

18. The bomb load of a Halifax is made into a train and towed to the dispersal point.

19. Carriers being fitted to 1,000-lb. bombs before hoisting them into their appointed position in the main bomb bay. The bombs are arranged in such a manner as to take their proper place in the "sticks."

20. A bomb winch operating through the roof of the bomb bay (the cabin floor) hoists the bombs into their racks.

22. While the Halifaxes are being prepared, the aircrews are "briefed" by the Wing Commander for the night's raid and the navigators work out their courses.

21. Containers of 30-lb. incendiaries being stowed in the port wing racks.

23. Wearing parachute harness and flotation jacket, the rear gunner checks the auxiliary ammunition chutes amidships.

24. The pilot takes his place at the controls and the Halifax takes off on another operation.

25. On their return the aircrews appreciate a hot cup of tea while telling their story.

26. The "Chancelight" is switched on if necessary to floodlight the landing runway.

27. Under two huge photographic maps of Hamburg and the Ruhr, the crews tell their story to the Intelligence Officer—a W.A.A.F. in this instance. 28. Meanwhile the Ruhr Valley Express is being overhauled once more.

RUHR VALLEY EXPRESS

2 Comfortably clad in shirts and shorts the aircrews listen to the briefing in the afternoon.

1 Names of aircraft captains are posted up on the operations board.

OPERATIONS

21/22 OCTOBER
CAPTAIN
FLIGHT to AIR BASE
OPERATIONS
RETURN to BASE

F/SGT CLARKE
SGT GOLBSTON
SGT GIBBONS
SGT WYATT
SGT DECLERCK
F/O KNOX
F/SGT GRIBBEN
F/SGT THOMAS

5 The navigator-bomb aimer in the front compartment

6 Top protection. The air gunner in the mid-upper or dorsal turret.

8 The operations officer keeps in touch with the aircraft by radio telephone.

9 In the light of dawn. A Halifax returning after delivering the "Mail."

10 The squadron gunnery officer in the rear turret. The reflector sight can be seen just above his hand on the controls.

11 Telling the story of the raid to the intelligence officer.

12 A polite translation would read, "We operate almost anywhere."

Mail Run

How Handley Page Halifaxes Reduced the Axis Ports in Libya Before and During the Great Westward Advance

3 After briefing, the crews forgather and the navigators work out their courses.

4 Night scene in the desert. A Halifax ready to take off along the flare path.

7 Standing by the Chancelight the signaller gives a waiting Halifax the O.K. for take-off.

"LAST night allied bombers attacked Tobruk and Benghazi. Large fires and explosions were observed among dock installations and on quays." Until the recapture of these towns by the Eighth Army this announcement was made so regularly that it passed almost unnoticed. Behind these words lay one of the most persistent, powerful and vital air offensives against the Axis lines of supply in the Middle East. It was carried out by Halifax bombers. Every night, week in and week out, hundreds of men flew through the darkness over a distance of 1,100 miles to drop hundreds of tons of bombs. The men who flew on these raids called them the "Night Mail Run." The "Mail Run" whittled away shipping, dock machinery, stores and dislocated the organisation of enemy-occupied ports. They hit him hard behind the lines and confused his supply.

THE EVOLUTION of the
form is told by these p
nose of the original Ha
in its intermediate form after
the right is the remodelled ar
Series IA. This view shows
Merlin 22. Of the full-leng
Series I and that be

[" Aeroplane " photographs

y Page Halifax in modern
Immediately below is the
On the left is the nose
oval of the turret and on
ed nose of the Halifax II
cowling of the Rolls-Royce
es, that above is of the
ws the Series IA.

"FEATHERED FLIGHT"

HALIFAX

"Aeroplane" photograph

Halifax Characteristics

HANDLEY-PAGE HALIFAX II Series Ia

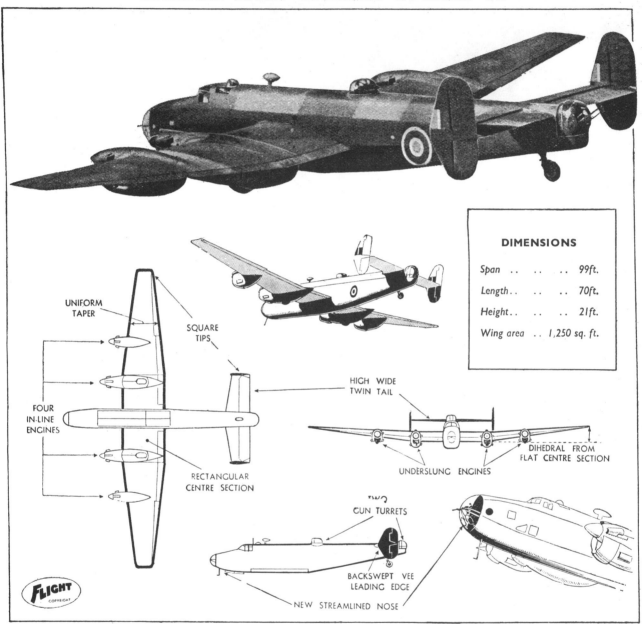

DIMENSIONS

Span	99ft.
Length..	70ft.
Height..	21ft.
Wing area ..	1,250 sq. ft.

UNIFORM TAPER

SQUARE TIPS

FOUR IN-LINE ENGINES

RECTANGULAR CENTRE SECTION

HIGH WIDE TWIN TAIL

DIHEDRAL FROM FLAT CENTRE SECTION

UNDERSLUNG ENGINES

GUN TURRETS

BACKSWEPT VEE LEADING EDGE

NEW STREAMLINED NOSE

IMPROVED bombing tactics and the need for greater speed has had its reflection in recent modifications to the detail design of the Handley-Page Halifax which have changed some of its recognition features.

It has been found that for night operations a nose turret is no longer really necessary, and that the gain in speed consequent upon the reduction in drag achieved by doing away with the nose turret is a distinct advantage.

The first change, which produced the Halifax II Series I, was the substitution of a blacked-in nose in place of the turret, thus presenting a rounded streamlined "entry" instead of the familiar "chin" of the Halifax I. A rounded bomb-aimer's panel was let into the underside of this new nose, and some of this version are in service without even dorsal armament, only the tail turret being retained.

This version, however, proved to be only an intermediate stage, for it has quickly been followed by the Halifax II Series Ia, on which a streamlined Perspex nose, containing a Vickers K gun on a flexible mounting, has supplanted the blacked-in type, and this is the version illustrated.

Yet another improvement in the Ia version is the substitution of a Boulton Paul four-gun power-operated dorsal turret for the two-gun turret fitted to the Mark I Halifax. This has not only strengthened the fire-power from this position, but it has reduced drag still further.

Other modifications of, perhaps, a minor character so far as practical recognition is concerned, are the abandonment of the fuel jettison pipes which previously protruded from the trailing-edge of the wings, and better streamlined engine nacelles, the inner pair of which now project slightly beyond the trailing-edge on the latest examples; this is shown in the small perspective sketch above.

The Halifax II is powered by Rolls-Royce Merlin XXII engines each developing 1,280 h.p., and its top speed in operational trim is now officially stated to be 261 m.p.h. at 19,500ft.

1. The two mechanics attending to the inner starboard Hercules give scale to the Halifax III.

2. This three-quarter rear view of the Halifax III shows the excellent fields of fire of the two 4-gun turrets.

Halifax Dev

Hercules Engines in Latest Version Heavy Bomber : Benefits of Incr

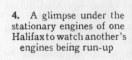

IN accordance with the engine interchangeability programme mapped out as far back as 1938, the Mark III version of the Handley Page Halifax is fitted with four 1,650 h.p. Bristol Hercules XVI engines in place of the Rolls-Royce Merlins which powered the Halifax I and II. The increased horse-power has, of course, resulted in improved performance, but security reasons forbid us from publishing exact details.

As would be expected, the take-off is improved and the rate of climb is better. The combination of the new engines and the addition of a further five feet to the wing span has stepped up the service ceiling by several thousand feet and, at the same time, the top speed has increased. The drag of the extra wing span has obviously been offset by the lower induced drag and the improved angle at which the new Halifax flies. This is one of the reasons for the greater speed.

Apart from the fitting of sleeve-valve engines there have also been several modifications to the defensive layout since the Halifax first went on operations early in 1941 The original Halifaxes had a two-gun turret in the nose, a two-gun dorsal turret and, like all our other heavies, a four-gun turret in the tail. The tail armament

4. A glimpse under the stationary engines of one Halifax to watch another's engines being run-up

6. High - explosive and incendiary bombs stowed away in the capacious bomb bay.

7. The gunner's point of view. An internal photograph of the Boulton Paul rear turret.

3. For comparison. An air photograph of the Halifax I which had a front turret, Rolls-Royce Merlin XX engines, and fins of smaller area.

5. The Hercules engines "fit in" nicely in the Halifax III and the whole presents a good-looking aircraft. Span is increased by 5ft. over the earlier Halifaxes.

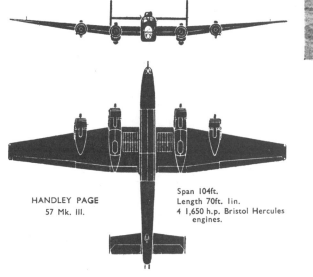

HANDLEY PAGE
57 Mk. III.

Span 104ft.
Length 70ft. 1in.
4 1,650 h.p. Bristol Hercules engines.

has remained the same and the dorsal turret has been increased in fire power by substituting a Defiant-type four-gun turret to replace the Hudson-type two-gun turret. All the turrets have been the electro-hydraulically operated types manufactured by Boulton Paul, Ltd. Defensive armament in the nose always presupposes that head-on attacks will have to be warded off. It has been found that these head-on attacks do not materialise during night bombing, and it was felt that the heavy front turret, which takes so many man-hours to make, was unnecessary. In the Mark II it was therefore removed and replaced by a streamlined nose of transparent plastic material. There was also modification within a modification, however, in

8. Relative positions. The navigator is on the same level but behind the pilot, while the radio operator is below.

Nicely proportioned, the Halifax III in its coat of night black looks every inch a modern night bomber. The new fins and rudders were fitted to the later Mark II, IA Halifaxes, as well as to the Hercules-engined Mark IIIs.

HALIFAX DEVELOPMENT

that a number of the Mark I Halifaxes had their front turrets removed and replaced by a closed-in nose with small windows and a bomb aimer's panel until the fully transparent noses could be supplied.

In the Mark II and III there has also been some alteration to the twin fins and rudders. There had been a slight tendency to yaw which has been quite cured by the fitting of fins of different shape and larger area. These increase damping in yaw and so reduce excessive rates of yaw during violent manœuvres. Co-incident with the change of engines in the Mark III the airscrews have also been changed. The liquid-cooled Merlin XXs in the Marks I and II had Rotol airscrews with blades of compressed wood, while the Hercules engines transmit their power through De Havilland hydromatic airscrews with metal blades.

First in the Field

The name of Handley Page, Ltd., has always been associated with large machines. It was this firm which produced our first twin-engined bomber, the Rolls-Royce Eagle engined 0/100, in 1915. A modified version of this, the 0/400, dropped the first bombs on Cologne in December, 1917. Again, it was Handley Page who produced our first four-engined bomber, the V/1500, in 1918. The V/1500 was designed to carry a 3,300 lb. bomb (one of which type can be seen in the Imperial War Museum) to drop on Berlin. Only the end of the 1914-18 war saved the Berliners from having a foretaste of things to come a quarter of a century later. A few nights ago a force of Halifax IIIs bombed Berlin and 100 per cent. of the force returned. Thus is the best Handley Page tradition maintained.

An interesting sidelight on the Halifax design is that Handley Pages have in mind a commercial type which will incorporate many of the sub-assemblies of the Halifax. It is the proud boast of the concern that in the 40-seater H.P.42 of 1930 they produced the first really commercial

The air bomber has an excellent panel through which to operate his bomb sight.

air liner. Certain it is that in the H.P.42 hundreds of thousands of passengers were carried in comfort—and not one of them was injured in any way.

HANDLEY PAGE'S LATEST : The Bristol Hercules - engined Halifax III above the clouds.

CONCENTRATED EFFORT : The second pilot's view of the starboard Bristol Hercules XVI engines as Halifax IIIs fly in formation.

NOW IN OPERATIONAL
SERVICE WITH THE
ROYAL AIR FORCE

HALIFAX III

POWERED BY
BRISTOL HERCULES
ENGINES

THE LATEST
HANDLEY PAGE
HEAVY BOMBER

"FLIGHT" PHOTO

HANDLEY PAGE LTD., LONDON   *Builders of Heavy Bombers since 1915*

["Aeroplane" photograph]

A FOURTH PART.—A close-up of the outboard port Bristol Hercules 14-cylinder air-cooled radial motor.

SINCE THE CLOSE of that fateful year 1940, Handley Page Halifax four-motor heavy bombers have been playing a large part in the destruction of the centres and lifelines of the German War Industry. Lacking the stately curves of contemporary thoroughbred aeroplanes, the Halifax was designed for speedy production, a factor which has proved of inestimable value to the Halifax group during the past five years.

In wartime, when maximum output is of first necessity, a bomber of such merit as the Halifax must needs be produced in great quantity, and so it was that the Halifax group was introduced to step up production. On March 20 Sir Frederick Handley Page called together and thanked the leaders of the Halifax group for their outstanding contribution, which totalled two-fifths of the complete bomber output of Great Britain. This Halifax group consists of four teams, the Fairey Aviation Co., the London Aircraft Production, Rootes Securities, and the English Electric Co., Ltd. Our story concerns the last-mentioned because, through the wholehearted co-operation of this company and the M.A.P., representatives of the Press were permitted to see for themselves the extent of production which has been achieved at one factory near Preston, Lancashire.

Arriving by motor coach from the nearby town, the Press party was first introduced to Sir George H. Nelson, Chairman and Managing Director of the English Electric Co., Ltd., and then speedily formed into groups to be shown round the factory.

The first thing to strike the unaccustomed ear was a high-pitched hooting sound reminiscent of a destroyer, which proved to be a satisfactory method of signalling to key personnel in the factory where in places the human voice would be lost above the noise of machinery.

Entering the airy and well-lighted Drawing Office, the visitor saw neatly spaced rows of tables which were used to design and estimate the tools and parts for the Halifax bomber. Passing through the massive Accounts Department the visitor came to the Costing and Progress Department, where, as in the former departments, both sexes are employed in the highly complicated task of keeping the flow of essential materials moving. A feature of the Preston works is that at any given moment the precise stage of construction of individual bombers

can be ascertained. Here the visitor was told that such a large Costing and Progress Department was needed because every part required in the manufacture of the Halifax was constructed in the factory, apart from certain proprietary rights such as the motors, undercarriage, gun turrets and instruments. This amounts to hundreds of thousands of small bits and pieces, besides the more impressive larger assemblies. These four departments are on the first floor of the main building, which had once been part of a Lancashire cotton mill.

Passing down steps one enters the noisy, warm, creative atmosphere of the Tool Room, which, because of its dimensions, rather belies its name. Here the English Electric Co. can be justly proud of stating that almost every part of the Halifax is machined in the one factory. Machinery from the United States stands side by side with British machinery. Some of the more important tooling machines are surrounded by blast walls. To one side girls are employed in checking the machined pieces before they are passed on to the respective departments.

As Sir George Nelson has stated, because the English Electric Co. had no connections with the broader aviation industry prior to 1938 it was essential to manufacture everything connected with the Halifax within the borders of the company. This step, which at the time was looked upon with disapproval by the Government, has since proved the faith and sound judgment displayed by the leaders in their team of workers.

Worthy of special merit is the giant rubber press operated by four women. This rubber die block press is a comparatively recent introduction to speed up delivery of a number of pressings which require curved cornerings and centre-pieces.

["Aeroplane" photograph]

MARRIAGE.—In the Final Assembly hangars the fuselage centre section is lowered into position and joined on to the front portion of the fuselage.

Produced by John Shaw and Sons, of Salford, this rubber press is capable of delivering a punch equal to 8,000 tons. The use of rubber sheeting not only assists in the curving but prevents shock damage to the material.

Leaving the Tool Room, the visitor was taken through the Heat Treatment Department which attends to the protective anodising of various parts. At one end of this department are the draw benches which deal with sheet metal strips to the order of 20 miles per week.

To the section that makes the most noise the credit must go to the Sheet Metal Working Department which hammers and cudgels metal into every shape desired.

From the Sheet Metal Department the eye perceives evidence of the desire to turn out everything, because farther on there is a section devoted to the production of every type of rivet, bolt and screw required in the finished article.

Passing on, women are more in evidence again in the Major Sub-assemblies Section which deals with the assembly of the fin, rudder and tailplane sections.

In the Machine Shop the English Electric Co. have developed a pneumatic single-shot riveter and, equally important, a foot-operated spot welder. These English Electric spot-welders are operated by women in the production of petrol tank sections. By using a foot-pedal the hands are left free to manœuvre the tank section, whereas in days gone by two operators were required.

In another section the visitor perceives the orderly lines of sub-assemblies, including fuselage sections, flaps and wings. Overhead runs the chain crane which lifts the completed sections to other finished parts farther along the line which, in turn, are being furnished with all the necessary impedimenta of flying controls and electrical equipment.

One of the highlights of the visit was the moulded transparencies section which comes under the neat if somewhat broad term of Plastics. Every transparency required in the

["Aeroplane" photograph]

ASSEMBLY LINES.—A general view of completed forward section of the Halifax fuselages, illustrating the attention given to floor space where every square foot is turned to good use.

HALIFAXES

Halifax is moulded in this well-lighted second-storey shop. The principle employed is that of heating Perspex to some 300 degrees F., and when in pliable state placing it over a moulding and securely clamping it down. Then the air is withdrawn from the underside and the pliable transparency settles down to fit snugly along the curved walls. After a period allowed for cooling off, the newly shaped Perspex is trimmed and passed over to women polishers who impart that much-envied crystal-clear surface. The dominating example of this procedure is the (Scanner) tear-drop-shaped fuselage canopy. This is well illustrated in one of the accompanying photographs. Usually four sections of Perspex are cemented together and placed on the hot bed. Felt is placed between the transparency and the electrically operated metal heating plate to prevent sticking. Over all is placed sheeting to contain the heated air. When in pliable state the workers carefully ease the plastic over the tear-drop-shaped cavity and quickly the clamping bars are pulled down and secured, the tear-drop-shaped railing on the clamps ensuring that the perimeter is securely held in place. The vacuum process is then applied and shortly after the weighted clamps are allowed to swing up and two men lift the canopy clear of the well, placing it in a further clamp to be neatly trimmed off ready for final cleaning up. At present this fuselage canopy is the World's largest single-piece moulding yet attempted for large-scale production.

Travelling back to the main production flooring, the eye gazes upon the Final Assembly lines, which leave the viewer with the definite impression of orderliness yet bulging produc-

MOULDING PROCESS.—A general view of the machinery used to mould a single Perspex part fitted to the rear underside of the Halifax. Men are seen here lifting out the complete covering, which will then be placed in clamps to be trimmed off ready for final cleaning.

PRESSING BUSINESS.—A feature of the Preston works is this giant rubber die block press which is used for the shaping of many airframe parts which require curved cornerings.

tion, where only sufficient space has been left for freedom of movement around the outside of the rapidly growing fuselage and wing sections. Above these lines go the overhead cranes which lift the completed sections to the exit, where 60-ft.-long Queen Mary trailers take them by road to the aerodrome some distance away to Final Assembly Sheds. Passing through the narrow streets, the forward part of the fuselage, complete with upper Boulton Paul four-gun turret, is on one truck, with the centre section of the wing complete with undercarriage (the whole being known in the works as the covered wagon), while on a second truck behind is the tail end of the fuselage and tail assembly.

In tall hangars of the English Electric aerodrome, the sections are married and the four Bristol Hercules radial motors bolted into position. Finally, the Rotol three-blade constant-speed airscrews are fitted.

All this time inspectors have been checking and rechecking, but at last the completed Preston-built Halifax is ready for flying tests. Before the test pilots take over, the bombers are wheeled over to another hangar to be filled with petrol and oil and then taken for compass-swinging tests and the rest of the innumerable last-minute adjustments.

The chief test pilot is Mr. J. D. Rose, who has been test-flying Preston-built bombers since the first Handley Page Hampden two-motor bomber was produced. When English Electric switched over to Halifax II four-motor bombers he flew the first in August, 1942. Since then, together with H. W. Easdown, who started in October, 1940, he has test-flown over 2,000 Halifax heavy bombers, and before that something like a thousand Hampden bombers.—a proud achievement.

The story of the Preston-built Halifax would not be complete without a brief reference to the aviation pedigree of the English Electric Co.

Aircraft design and construction was started in 1911 at Coventry (Coventry Ordnance Works; Ltd.), and in 1912

an aeroplane was built for the Military Trials. Orders were received for the construction of various military types, including the B.E.8a, which was in production when the last War broke out. At the same period the Phœnix Dynamo Manufacturing Co., Ltd., of Bradford, was producing the Short N2b anti-submarine seaplane. Other types built at Coventry included the R.E.7 bomber and R.E.8 and B.E.12a in 1916. In parallel, the Phœnix works at Bradford produced training aeroplanes, including the Maurice Farman Longhorn. In 1917, two experimental Armstrong Whitworth Quadruplanes were built, but proved unsuccessful. In 1917, at Preston, the Dick, Kerr and Co., Ltd., and the United Electric Car Co., Ltd., began building large biplane flying-boats for the Royal Naval Air Service. These were known as the F.3 and F.5, later to be followed by the P.5 Phœnix Cork flying-boat.

In 1918 the Coventry works were engaged in building Sopwith Snipe single-seat fighters, and the Bradford and Preston works concentrated on flying-boats on a large scale. Shortly after the war all the companies were amalgamated under the title of the English Electric Co., Ltd. The best-known post-War types were the Kingston Marks I-III biplane flying-boats, and the diminutive Wren monoplane of 1923 powered by a 3 h.p. A.B.C. 398 c.c. motor, and the Ayr flying-boat which was designed to test the possibilities of using partially submerged lower planes in place of wing-tip floats.

By March, 1926, the English Electric Co., Ltd., had decided to retire from the aeronautical field because of the lack of orders and the need to concentrate on rolling stock.

When the shadow factory scheme came into operation before the present War, the E.E.C. extended its Preston works and started all over again—this time producing Hampdens.

Now that Sir George Nelson has stated that the English Electric Co. is to remain in the aviation field we can expect to hear more of it in the future, and no doubt we shall see parent designed aeroplanes which will equal the reputation of the Phœnix flying-boats of the last War.

SPOT WELDER.—Designed and constructed by the English Electric Company Ltd. is this electric spot-welder which speeds up production by the use of foot pedals for operation, leaving both hands free.

Handley Page Civil Programme

Most prominent feature of the civil Halifax (above) is the "pannier" in place of the bomb bay. Below is an artist's impression of the Hermes cargo version being loaded.

Converted Halifax Bomber Ready to Fill the Interim Period : A Cargo Version of the Hermes Passenger Carrier

THINGS are moving fast in British civil aviation in spite of the uncertainty caused by the fact that the White Paper is still waiting to be "implemented" and the imminence of the general election may cause a complete change of Government policy. Recent civil types announced and described in this journal are the de Havilland Dove, the Short Shetland flying boat, and the Vickers Viking, while some months ago (October 19th, 1944) we described and illustrated the Handley Page Hermes passenger carrier.

The Handley Page company now announces two more civil types : a passenger conversion of the Halifax bomber and a freight version of the Hermes. Both are powered by four Bristol Hercules engines (not identical versions, however), each giving more than 1,650 h.p. for take-off, so that an interesting comparison can be made between the converted bomber and the out-and-out civil type. The former has a normal gross weight of 65,000 lb., while the latter weighs 75,000 lb. loaded. The Halifax has a wing area of 1,275 sq. ft.; that of the Hermes is 1,408 sq. ft. Thus the two wing loadings are 51 lb./sq. ft. and 53 lb./sq. ft. respectively. The corresponding power loadings (based

on 1,650 h.p. per engine for take-off) are 9.85 lb./h.p. and 11.35 lb./h.p. respectively. The combined loadings (wing loadings multiplied by power loadings) are 500 and 600 respectively. Dr. Edward P. Warner has laid it down that for maximum economy the combined loading should be about 300, so both these Handley Page types exceed this figure by a considerable amount, the Hermes by 100 per cent.

Cruising Speed and Consumption

An interesting sidelight is thrown on aircraft design by the fact that in spite of its higher combined loading, the Hermes cruises at a most economical cruising speed of 194 m.p.h., while the corresponding figure for the Halifax is 210 m.p.h. at 15,000ft. and 200 m.p.h. at 10,000ft., not a very great difference. The larger machine, therefore, must be proportionately "cleaner." This is brought out much more strikingly by the consumption figures.

The makers have not provided figures of miles per gallon, but these can be calculated from the data given in the tables. Maximum range for the Halifax on normal tankage is 2,530 miles, the tankage being 2,190 gallons. This, there-

Two of the eleven passengers of the Halifax have seats convertible into berths (below).

Unturreted. The civil version of the Halifax (above) has a maximum level speed of 320 m.p.h.

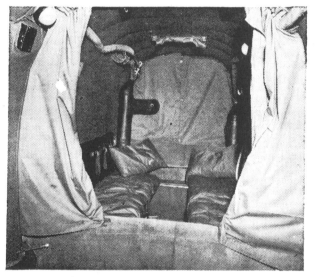

fore, represents an average fuel consumption of 1.156 miles per gallon. The corresponding figure for the Hermes is 1.175 miles per gallon or, for all practical purposes, the same consumption, although the Hermes is a much larger and heavier machine. In other words, the type designed initially for commercial work is a good deal more efficient, aerodynamically, than the converted bomber.

Ranges and Payloads

Even this figure does not convey the vast difference in commercial efficiency of the two types. The pay load is the item most closely concerned. It is illuminating to find, on examining the two tables of data, that the civil Halifax at 2,530 miles' range carries a payload of 7,750 lb., whereas the Hermes carries a payload of 13,000 lb. over a range of 2,600 miles. That difference illustrates clearly the greater efficiency of the civil type. The engines in the two types are not identical, but their differences are not sufficient to account for the remarkable advantage of the Hermes

Converted Halifax
Four Hercules Engines

Wing Span - - - 104ft.
Normal Gross Wt. 65,000 lb.

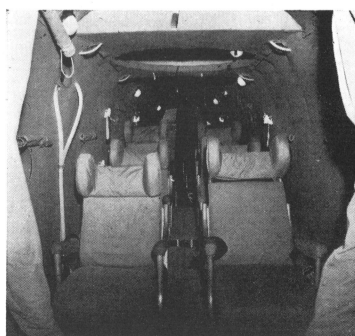

Elbowroom is not plentiful inside the civil Halifax, and it would appear that passengers will have to walk sideways along the gangway.

Spaciousness inside the Hermes. Transport of fire-fighting equipment might well be one of the functions of this machine.

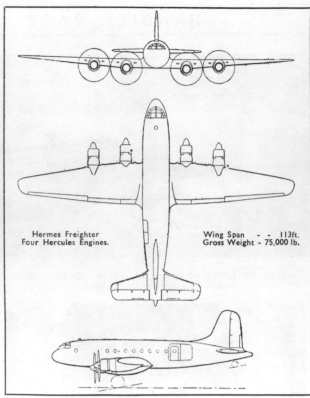

Hermes Freighter
Four Hercules Engines.

Wing Span - - 113ft.
Gross Weight - 75,000 lb.

from an economy point of view. First cost will, of course, enter into the calculations to a marked extent, but the Halifax would have to be very cheap indeed to compete over a period of several years with the Hermes.

Of course, the comparison is not quite fair because the Halifax is a bomber converted into a passenger carrier while the Hermes is a freighter. The table shows, however, that of the basic equipped weight of the Halifax of 40,600 lb., 2,850 lb. is accounted for by crew and removable equipment. Thus, leaving the odd 850 lb. for the crew, there is only 2,000 lb. to be transferred to the payload side of the ledger. In the figures quoted above, this would mean increasing the payload of the Halifax from 7,750 lb. to 9,750 lb., still a long way below the freight load, for the same range, of the Hermes.

On the principle that half a loaf is better than no bread, the Halifax may well fill what would otherwise have been an awkward gap. It is available almost at once, and there should be no difficulty about spares. So let us see what it has to offer. The space in the fuselage has been furnished to accommodate 11 passengers. Nine of them

are provided with armchair seats while, as the makers' description somewhat frankly states, the other two are accommodated "in a comfortable compartment that is readily convertible into sleeping berths." The tacit admission that the other nine are not very comfortable is borne out by the photograph, which shows a very narrow gangway between the rows of seats. However, the Halifax is intended to serve during a period when speed of travel over long distances may be deemed more important than luxurious comfort.

Halifax Cargo Capacity

The most ingenious feature of the converted Halifax is the cargo "pannier" slung under the portion of the fuselage where is the bomb bay in the military machine.

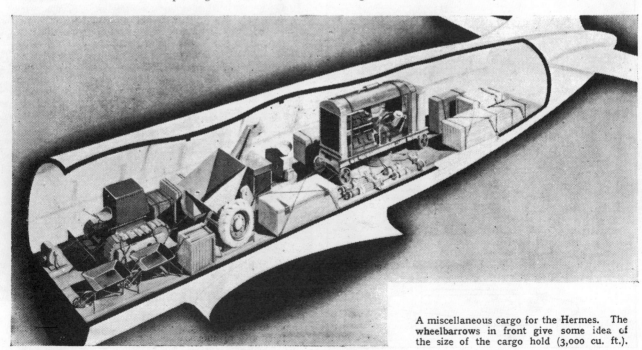

A miscellaneous cargo for the Hermes. The wheelbarrows in front give some idea of the size of the cargo hold (3,000 cu. ft.).

HALIFAX TRANSPORT
Four Bristol Hercules Engines
General Data

Wing span	104 ft. 0 in.
Wing area	1,275 sq. ft.
Tare weight	37,750 lb.
Removable equipment and crew	2,850 lb.
Fuel (normal tanks)	2,190 Imp. gals.
Fuel (long-range tanks)	2,880 ,,
Oil	128 gals.
Basic equipped weight	40,600 lb.
Engines ... ... 4 Bristol Hercules of 1,650 h.p.
Airscrews ... de Havilland Hydromatic three-bladers, fully feathering.

Performance

Max. level speed	320 m.p.h.
Max. weak-mixture cruising at 10,000ft.	260 ,,
,, ,, ,, 15,000ft.	270 ,,
Economical cruising speed at 10,000ft.	200 ,,
,, ,, ,, 15,000ft.	210 ,,

Range and Load

At 65,000 lb. gross weight (landing weight, 55,000 lb.) :

Max load	12,100 lb.
Range with max. load	1,810 miles
Range with 10,000 lb. load	2,150 ,,
Max. range (normal tanks)	2,530 ,,
Load for max. range (normal tanks)	7,750 lb.
Max. range (long-range tanks)	3,510 miles
Load for max. range (long-range tanks) ...	2,500 lb.

At 68,000 lb. gross weight (landing weight, 57,000 lb.) :

Max. load	14,100 lb.
Range with max. load	1,860 miles
Range with 12,500 lb. load	2,120 ,,
Max. range (normal tanks)	2,420 ,,
Load for max. range (normal tanks)	10,750 lb.
Max. range (long-range tanks)	3,360 miles
Load for max. range (long-range tanks) ...	5,450 lb

HERMES CARGO CARRIER
Four Bristol Hercules Engines
(over 1,650 h.p. for take-off)
General Data

Wing span	113 ft. 0 in.
Wing area	1,408 sq. ft.
Bare weight	37,642 lb.
Normal fuel capacity...	2,574 gals.
Long-range capacity	2,874 ,,
Oil capacity	120 ,,
Max. take-off weight	75,000 lb.
Landing weight	70,000 ,,

Performance

Max. level speed	337 m.p.h.
Max. weak-mixture cruising speed	284 ,,
Most economical cruising speed	194 ,,
Rate of climb (sea level)	1,010 ft./min.
Time to 10,000ft.	10 mins.

Range and Payload

		At 240 m.p.h.	At 194 m.p.h.
Range with 18,000 lb. load	...	1,600 miles	1,745 miles
,, ,, 16,000 lb. ,,	...	1,880 ,,	2,000 ,,
,, ,, 13,000 lb. ,,	...	2,340 ,,	2,600 ,,
Max. range (normal tanks) ...	...	2,700 ,,	3,030 ,,
Corresponding load		10,720 lb.	10,720 lb.
Max. range (long-range tanks)	...	3,040 miles	3,445 miles
Corresponding load		8,240 lb.	8,240 lb.

This pannier can carry loads (fairly dense, one supposes) of up to 8,000 lb. weight. If all 11 passengers are carried, with their luggage, over the maximum range with normal tanks of 2,530 miles, they will not leave all of the 8,000 lb. load available for the pannier, but only some 5,250 lb. However, even this would be an acceptable payload if carried in the form of mails. If the gross weight is increased from 65,000 lb. to 68,000 lb., as it can be, the pannier could be loaded to full capacity. Such a combination would, therefore, be quite useful on many of the Empire routes. The table shows that even on much longer ranges the payload is still very substantial at the overload gross weight of 68,000 lb. Hatches fore and aft enable the pannier to be loaded and unloaded from below, and as the pannier itself is raised and lowered by hoists in the aircraft, it would be possible for standardised loads to be placed in readiness in a pannier, ready for transfer as a complete unit to the aircraft, thus making possible a quick "turn-round" at airports, one pannier being unshipped and the waiting one hoisted on board to take its place.

Hermes Freighter

In the cargo version of the Handley Page Hermes, the main structural difference is in the floor. The passenger machine, it may be recollected, has a pressure cabin. This of course, is not needed for the freighter, and instead there is a specially constructed floor designed to support the very heavy concentrated loads which it may be expected to carry. Lashing points, in the form of large substantial rings, are provided at frequent intervals on the floor and on the fuselage walls. When not in use these rings are located in channels so as to lie flush with the surface.

The main cargo compartment is more than 40ft. long and has a capacity of 3,000 cu. ft. In addition there are two holds in the underside of the fuselage, under the floor. These have a combined capacity of 190 cu. ft., and have loading hatches accessible from the outside. The forward hold can also be reached from inside the machine during flight.

Externally the cargo Hermes differs, but little from the passenger version. The most noticeable change is the fitting of large doors on the port side. These doors provide an entrance measuring 9ft. 4in. by 5ft. 9in. for the loading of bulky freight. Loading can be carried out by means of a ramp, gantry or mechanical loading truck.

Speed–effect on Range

Reference has already been made to the efficiency of the Hermes from the point of view of load-carrying capacity as compared with the converted Halifax. From the table of data an additional fact emerges: the effect of increasing the cruising speed is relatively small. When the machine is fitted with long-range tanks and carrying a payload of 8,240 lb., the maximum range is only decreased from 3,445 miles to 3,040 miles by increasing the average cruising speed from 194 m.p.h. to 240 m.p.h. That means, of course, that if a particular cargo is wanted in a great hurry, the operator can oblige the shipper without incurring a prohibitive fuel cost thereby. On the other hand, where punctuality is essential, there is the possibility of increasing the cruising speed on any particular trip in order to fight strong head winds.

That the Hermes will have to be a "mainliner" appears obvious from the wing loading of 53 lb./sq. ft. A long concrete runway would seem to be essential for the take-off; and at the maximum permissible landing weight of 70,000 lb. the wing loading is still about 50 lb./sq. ft., at which loading the touch-down will have to be made somewhere in the 100 m.p.h. neighbourhood. Since, however, the machine is most likely to be used on fairly long stages, it will probably not very often be required to land at a weight of 70,000 lb. It seems probable that the stages will usually be of some 1,500 miles, during which something like 11,250 lb. of fuel will have been consumed, thereby bringing the landing weight down to 63,750 lb., or a wing loading of approximately 45 lb./sq. ft. Even at this relatively long range, the payload will be in the neighbourhood of nine tons.

35,000 AIRMEN TRAINED IN AUSTRALIA

MESSAGES of congratulation on the Australian share in the Empire Air Training Scheme, now closed down, have been exchanged between the Minister for Air of the Commonwealth of Australia, Mr. A. S. Drakeford, and the Secretary of State for Air, Sir Archibald Sinclair. Mr. Drakeford's message reveals that Australia provided 35,000 trained air crew under the scheme.

In the course of his message Mr. Drakeford said: "A magnificent chapter of history has ended with the closing down of the Empire Air Training Scheme. The fact that the Dominions are now able to discontinue large-scale training tells its own story of accomplishment. . . . The scheme enabled the Empire to turn alarming numerical inferiority into overwhelming superiority in numbers and quality of air crew."

Halifax A-IX Airborne Transport

New Version of Handley Page Bomber : Bomb Bay to Carry Fuel or Supplies

Illustrated by "Flight" photographs

MEETING the requirements of both the R.A.F. and the Airborne Forces, Handley Pages have produced a specialised version of the Halifax and designated it the A-IX.

Although designed primarily for use by the Airborne Forces, it can still be operated as a bomber or transport. A crew of six is carried, and there is accommodation for 16 fully-equipped paratroops and two dispatchers.

The outline of the aircraft is scarcely altered, but internally there are a number of innovations. The rear turret, which formerly carried four 0.303in. machine guns, is now replaced by a Boulton Paul D turret mounting two 0.5in. guns. There is no mid-upper gun position.

An inward-opening main entrance door also provides the paratroop exit. The dimensions of the door are 33in. by 59in., and it is operated by a hand lever on the port wall of the fuselage. Two rails take the static lines from the paratroops' canopies and, after a drop, these lines are hauled aboard by winches attached to the rear spar. On the ceiling of the fuselage, immediately above the jumping aperture, there is a signalling panel operated by the air bomber who "aims" the paratroops or supplies. All the crew and paratroop positions have controlled

heating available to counteract cold weather or high-flying conditions. Considerable supplies of oxygen are also carried. The batteries of oxygen bottles are in the floor, below the flight engineer's position.

A streamline pannier may be fitted into the bomb bay to carry 8,000 lb. of military equipment or, if required, long-range fuel tanks can take the place of the pannier.

Two large-capacity "J" type inflatable dinghies are provided for the safety of the crew, and stowage space is available for "K" dinghies for both crew and troops.

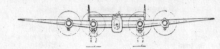

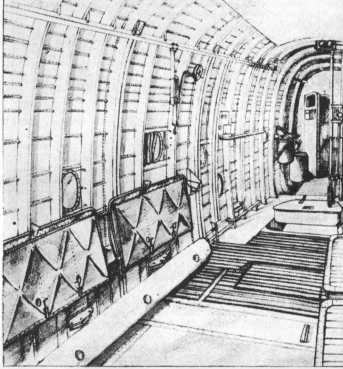

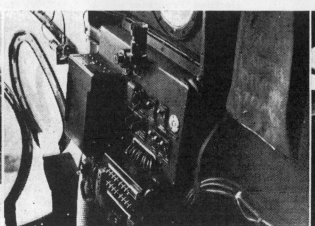

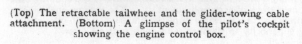

(Top) The retractable tailwheel and the glider-towing cable attachment. (Bottom) A glimpse of the pilot's cockpit showing the engine control box.

The air bomber's panel with its row of bomb selector switches is on the starboard side of the clear-vision nose. The release switch is stowed in a spring clip.

The exterior of the A-IX shows little change, but the drawing of the interior illustrates the many changes in internal economy which have taken place. After seeing the sheet metal seats, no one can say that our paratroops go to war in comfort.

Handley Page Halifax A-IX
Max. speed (full load at 22,000ft.) 320 m.p.h.
Range (full load at economical
  cruising) ... ... 2,080 miles
Max. load ... ... 8,699 lb.
Four 1675 h.p. Bristol Hercules XVI engines.

(Below) The massive-looking entrance door in the half-open position. It is raised and lowered by a lever on the fuselage wall.

Escape hatches are provided in the roof. The D.F. aerial can be seen on the roof.

(Centre) Two 0.5in. machine guns are now carried in the tail. The elevators are shown in the "parked" up position.
(Bottom) Part of the store of oxygen bottles.

Up from the deep

S for Sugar skimmed low over the icy waters of Fotten Fjord off Trondheim Fjord on the mountainous northwest coast of Norway. Somewhere ahead lay the 45,000-ton German *Bismarck*-class battleship *Tirpitz* which was lurking in the fjords awaiting the right moment to join the developing U-boat campaign in the Atlantic as a raider. The attacks on our vital North Atlantic convoys had to be

stayed until America could really get going and help to provide effective counter measures. *Tirpitz* had to be disabled and thereby prevented from becoming one more threat to Atlantic shipping. As a prelude, the submarine pens and dry-dock at St. Nazaire—the only dry dock on the French Atlantic coast big enough to take the giant *Tirpitz*—was disabled by the daring commando raid of March 27-28, 1942.

But *Tirpitz* must be stopped from leaving her Norwegian hide-out. This was the brief given to Bomber Command. It was the brief which took one particular Halifax from Morayshire in Scotland on a one-way trip across the North Sea at 250 feet.

Lancasters led by former Imperial Airways pilot Wing Commander D. C. T. Bennett (who also made several flights in Mercury, the pick-a-back seaplane, from flying boat Maia) had already gone in and bombed *Tirpitz* from 4,000ft in the clear moonlit sky, and now 35 Squadron's Halifax Mk. IIs were to attempt a low-level kill. The mission was more than usually dangerous: moonlight meant they could be seen. It also meant

Photograph by Bjorn Olsen

heavy and well-aimed flak. And behind the German battleship the cliffs rose steeply into the night sky. So steep were these cliffs that the Lancasters had aimed for the rock so that their relatively small bombs, mines and depth charges would roll down the precipice to damage the ship below the water-line.

Only 12 days out of the English Electric factory where, as W1048, she was one of a batch of 181 Halifax bombers, S for Sugar was on her very first operational mission with a new crew. Suddenly she flew into heavy flak and, as she dropped her mines, a sickening thud indicated that she had been hit—hard. The starboard outer engine was a ball of fire. Ahead the cliffs and a maximum-boost climb. She managed to clear the rock but it was obvious that she would never make it back to base at Kinloss. Twenty-four year old Fg Off Don McIntyre searched the arctic night for somewhere to land as the Halifax lost altitude. The moonlight showed a frozen lake ahead and, as this was the only level area to be found in the tree-clad hills, McIntyre aimed his crippled machine at the ice. They made a smooth enough wheels-up landing—and then skidded wildly and uncontrollably in a spume of icy crystals. When they came to rest, the crew of six scrambled out safely, the only injury being to the Flight Engineer who broke his ankle. As they slithered away from the Halifax, the heat from the blazing engine melted the ice and, as they watched, she cracked her way through and was gone, only a thin pall of smoke remaining above the black hole in the white surface of Lake Hoklingen. It was a quarter to one on the morning of April 28, 1942.

For 31 years, the dark, still, cold waters of Hoklingen preserved the war relic. Meanwhile, as with so many famous aircraft types, Halifax bombers went for scrap, were melted down and made back into saucepans and ploughshares. One day, somewhere, the last Halifax was sawn up and thrown into the furnace. The breed had vanished. Whether by acci-

Top left, close-up view of the nose turret turned to port. Above, the cockpit, slightly the worse for wear after 31 years under water. Below left, the port inner Merlin engine and below, the fin flash, roundel, squadron code and call sign TL-S and the service number W1048 are still clear. The fabric on all control surfaces has, however, rotted away. The photograph on the previous pages shows the Halifax just before it was winched the last few feet to the shore.

Bjorn Olsen

dent or intent, the Royal Air Force had paid its last respects to one of Bomber Command's early mainstays. And as so often, preservation is a line of thought only generated after there is nothing left to preserve.

But there was still a Halifax which everybody had forgotten—S for Sugar. On June 19, 1973, a 16-man team of RAF and civil divers led by Sgt Dave Walker of RAF West Drayton travelled to Lake Hoklingen, located the aircraft in 90ft of water, and began salvage operations. Other than the flak and fire damage to the starboard outer engine, the aircraft was found to be in a remarkably good state of preservation. Lying at such a depth in a relatively still and largely freshwater lake had caused surprisingly little deterioration to the structure.

Fabric had rotted from the control surfaces, cabin transparencies had distorted and paint was peeling, but other than that, the one-mission "Halibag" was repairable. At 14.10 hrs on June 30, S for Sugar surfaced and breathed air for the first time for 31 years, two months and two days.

The aircraft was lifted using fifty-one empty oil drums. During the initial lift, the damaged starboard outer wing and engine broke off but were recovered separately. Airframe parts made of magnesium alloy had corroded, but the duralumin structure was found to be practically as new. There was very little in the way of rust and the recovery team noted that screws, nuts and bolts could be undone without undue effort. Even more astonishing was that the elec-

trical wiring was undamaged and when a battery was connected, the instrument panel lights worked. Shoes, parachutes, overalls, gloves and first aid kits were all present, as were the observer's log and charts of the Northern approaches to Scotland which, in their understandable haste to abandon ship, the crew had not been able to destroy.

Now beached silently in the rushes, the old war veteran awaits careful dismantling by a detachment of engineers from No. 71 MU followed by a slow and reverent journey home. After restoration she will take her rightful place alongside the Spitfire, Defiant and Wellington at the RAF Museum, Hendon. The Museum already has on display a Gladiator rescued from a similar situation.   **A.W.O-H**

Bjorn Olsen

Finger trouble

The author joined up in February 1942 at the age of 18, imagining that he was well on the way towards becoming a fighter pilot. He was rejected as aircrew by a medical board and settled for Flight Mechanic (Engine). He served with 44 Squadron, 619 Squadron and 346 Squadron, and we join him during service with No 1658 Heavy Conversion Unit at Riccall, Yorkshire, servicing Halifaxes. He recalls incidents tragic and light during his twelve-month period with the unit.

Our job on a conversion unit was nothing like as pleasant as on a squadron. The work was harder, there was nothing obvious to show for it, no bombs to paint up, no feeling of pride when hearing on the radio "Aircraft of Bomber Command last night attacked targets in the Ruhr, much damage was done", and no parties with the aircrew. On the credit side there was a regular day off and to some extent, the feeling, which the C.O. and the Flight Commander did their best to foster, that as con. units went we were pretty good, and that we were the best flight on the unit. The only other compensation we had was a good deal of light relief provided by the inexperience of the aircrews, which, although it could easily have had tragic results, very seldom did, and possibly because of this caused us much amusement.

Perhaps the classic example of this kind of thing was the character who came back from a night cross-country and, when asked if there were any snags, said that "George" (the autopilot) seemed a bit queer. He went on to say that he had trimmed the aircraft and engaged "George", and after some time, during which "George" behaved perfectly, he left him in charge while he went back down the fuselage to answer a call of nature. Upon his return he found the aircraft about 1,000ft higher and 10° off course. We laughed and laughed, and he, very puzzled, inquired why. We told him that owing to the impossibility of obtaining a certain spare part for "George" we disconnected "him" altogether when this particular component gave trouble and wired the control in the off position. His was one of the aircraft on which this had been done.

When the pilot had got over his fright, which took some time, he too saw. the funny side, and said that he had meant to mention that he had found the on/off control very stiff to operate, but once he had moved it, it seemed O.K! He had, in fact, not a leg to stand on, had the matter turned out to be serious, as there was an entry in red ink in the Form 700 which he had signed before flight.

We called this kind of thing "finger trouble", and we became quite expert at reading through a list of snags and spotting which ones were genuine and which were the result of "finger trouble".

It is perhaps an interesting facet of my nature that the mention of Lancasters or any of my Lancaster stations immediately brings to my mind a picture of aircraft taking off on "ops" on a nice summer evening, but mention of Halifaxes or Riccall summons up a picture of crashed aeroplanes and engines in various states of disrepair. Why this should be I don't know, but it is possibly because there was far more flying at Riccall, and therefore more "incidents", particularly as the aircrews were less experienced both in flying and engine handling.

However, it is a remarkable tribute to the rugged construction of the aircraft and to the guardian angels concerned, that during the ten months or so I was at Riccall we only lost two crews, although we had perhaps 20 or more prangs of varying severity.

By STEPHEN REW

One of these two "fatals" could have happened to any aircraft; on a night cross-country in bad weather, the crew became lost and flew into a mountain with catastrophic results. The other, however, was due to the complexity of the fuel system and the inexperience of the aircrew. It was laid down that the aircraft had to land on one particular set of four fuel tanks, and the cocks had to be operated in a certain sequence, otherwise there was a risk of getting air locks in the fuel system. On this occasion an aircraft was returning from a night cross-country, and the flight engineer went down the fuselage and operated the fuel cocks to change on to the right set of tanks. Unfortunately he got the sequence wrong and the two port engines cut, owing to an air lock. The aircraft was turning to port at the time, to start its final approach, and at about 500ft the port wing dropped uncontrollably, the aircraft side-slipping into the ground about a mile from the runway. It blew up on impact and there were no survivors.

Apart from these two crews, nobody was even seriously injured during my time on the station, with the result that all the other prangs took on a rather comic aspect. For example, there was the chap who, when coming in to land one evening at dusk, selected the appropriate fuel tanks, but unfortunately overlooked the fact that he had already almost emptied them. He then decided to overshoot because he was too high. He therefore slammed the throttles wide open, but instead of a thunderous roar, all that happened was an " 'orrible 'ush" as all four engines cut. The powerless kite staggered across the aerodrome, missing our flight office by inches, and hit the deck just by one of our dispersals. It bounced over a couple of hedges and a road into a field, and hit again on one wheel and a wing tip. There was a terrifying grinding, crashing noise, which seemed to go on for hours, and finally silence. We rushed across, expecting to find seven mangled bodies, instead of which we found bits of aeroplane scattered all over the field and seven rather startled men wandering about in flying kit, wondering how they got there.

One of the great virtues of the Halifax was that when it pranged it snapped off clean at the joints between the sub-assemblies, and the various sub-sections went their separate ways complete with whoever happened to be inside them. The usual pattern of breakage was for the engines to fall out first, then the nose section including Pilot, Engineer, Navigator, Wireless Op, and Bomb Aimer, then the outer wings and the tail unit including the rear gunner, and finally the rear fuselage complete with mid-upper gunner, leaving only a short length of fuselage with the inner eight or ten feet of the wings attached. Each section was usually relatively undamaged apart from being a bit dented and battered, with the result that the occupants, having undone their straps, could usually walk out of their respective components.

Over to sleeve-valves

I had not been on the unit long before we converted from Mk. IIs and Vs with Merlins to Mark IIIs and VIs with Bristol Hercules sleeve-valve engines. We had had plenty of snags on Merlins, largely owing to the installation, and we greeted the change with great joy, having heard tales of the great reliability of "Hercs".

Alas for our hopes! In the event we were rather worse off with "Hercs" than with Merlins, although, in the light of subsequent knowledge, I think this was largely due to the prevailing operating conditions:— inexperienced aircrews, second-hand aircraft, our own inexperience in servicing them, and the continual thrashing which they endured on circuits and bumps.

One of their more diverting habits was to occasionally discard an entire propeller and reduction gear assembly in flight, although even this was preferred by the aircrews to the Merlin version's alternative of throwing a propeller blade away.

One reason they did not endear themselves to us was that when the engines had been standing for more than four hours, they had to be turned over by hand for two complete revolutions before attempting to start up. This was a job involving some very hard work with a handle very much like an overgrown car starting handle, which had to be turned about 20 times or more to turn the engine once, and after turning a couple of engines over one was cursing "Mr Bristol" and all his works.

Another weakness was the frequent oiling-up of spark plugs, necessitating changing the six plugs in the three bottom cylinders, replacing the cowling and running the engine, hoping that it had been one of the bottom six plugs causing the trouble. Nine times out of ten it was, but the tenth time we would have to remove the cowlings again and change the remaining 22 plugs.

This trouble was largely caused by letting the engine idle too long when taxiing, instead of opening up each engine at fairly frequent intervals. The symptom was usually a mag drop, but sometimes the engine would refuse to open up, and it would bang, spit back, and simply refuse to play.

There was, however, a strictly unofficial technique which would some-times achieve the desired object, and I shall never forget the first time I used it. I was on night flying when control rang up to say that one of our kites was coming in off circuits and bumps with engine trouble. I went out, guided him into dispersal and went up into the cockpit, while the engines were still running, to enquire what was wrong. The skipper said that he didn't know, but the starboard inner would not open up, and he showed me by opening the throttle slowly. When the revs reached 1,900, it started banging and spitting like the clappers, and further opening up merely made it worse.

Drastic measures

As it was about 2 a.m. and very cold, I did not fancy changing plugs, so I decided to try and clear the trouble by "other means". If I could once get the engine up to full power, I could coarsen pitch on the propeller, which would make the engine labour like a car going up hill, and probably run hot enough to burn the oil off the plugs.

I moved the throttle lever slowly up to 1,850 r.p.m. and then jerked it forward about an inch. The engine hiccupped and then picked up at about 2,100 r.p.m. I went on opening up, but at 2,350 r.p.m. the banging and spitting recurred, and the same trick did not work again. The prospect of a plug change loomed closer, colder, and even more unpleasant. I decided to make one last, despairing effort. I throttled back to idling and slammed the throttle lever forward as hard as I could. The engine coughed and spluttered like a mortally insulted retired colonel, but after several seconds it found itself at full power, without quite knowing how it got there. I eased it back to the "gate" (maximum power for long periods), and then grasped the propeller control lever and moved it firmly from "max r.p.m." to "min r.p.m.". The rev counter fell from 2,650 to about 1,600 while the boost pressure fell only slightly.

The effect was startling. The exhaust pipes and manifold changed from dull red and black respectively to brilliant red and dull red, due to the extra heat, and the engine sounded as if it was being attacked by half-a-dozen men with pneumatic drills. I gazed at it somewhat awestruck for a few seconds, wondering how long I dare let this state of affairs continue, when the flight engineer tapped me on the shoulder and pointed to the cylinder temperature gauge, which was going up like a rocketing pheasant. When it reached the absolute maximum permitted, I looked away, counted five, and then put the propeller lever back to "max", throttling back to 1,200 r.p.m.

The engine soon cooled off, so I did a normal run-up and checked the mags. There was hardly a flicker from the gauge. I asked the pilot if he was satisfied, and he said he was. I told

him that what I had done was strictly unofficial, and that he had not seen me do it. He nodded assent, and I left the aircraft, waved him out on to the peri-track and went back to the flight office.

In the brashness of youth and inexperience, I thought I had been jolly clever, but with the enlightenment of years I am not so sure. Admittedly, I got away with it then and on subsequent occasions, but I was taking a fair risk of damaging the engine, and it is a tribute to "Mr Bristol" that no appreciable damage ever resulted, for this was not uncommon practice.

Scrap collection

Another snag to which we found Hercs were prone caused us no end of fun and games, particularly the first time it occurred. An aircraft came back with an engine feathered, and all the pilot could tell us was that it had suddenly started "banging", accompanied by flashes of flame from under the cowling. We tried to run it, but as soon as it fired, sure enough, it banged and there were flashes of flame from under the cowling. We uncowled it and looked round, and found one of the cylinder inlet pipes from the supercharger broken, so we replaced it, cowled up and tried to run again.

The same thing happened, and when we looked the pipe we had just replaced had gone again. We then checked the timing and the ignition harness with no result, and changed both magnetos without success. Then we changed the ignition harness, and in desperation the carburettor, but still no joy. We then stood back and scratched our heads. Finally the sergeant said "Go and take the scavenger filter out". This filtered the oil after it had been round the engine and before it went back to the oil tank. We asked him what his idea was, and he replied "I don't know really, but it might tell us something. Anyway, we can't just stand here doing nothing."

We removed the filter, and a gallon or so of oil gushed out and into the bucket accompanied by queer dull clanging noises. We carefully poured the oil away and there, at the bottom of the bucket, was an enormous collection of assorted ironmongery, balls, rollers, and bits of cages from bearings, teeth off gear wheels and all manner of things.

To give the sergeant his due, he did not say "I told you so", but only "Fair enough, change the engine", which we did, washing out the oil system as well, and that was that. Some time later, after the engine had been stripped and examined, it was found that a nut in the sleeve-valve drive mechanism had come adrift and dropped into the timing gears, breaking a few teeth off here and there, and these had found their way into other parts of the engine, including the main bearings. Subsequently, when similar symptoms manifested themselves, we took the filter out straight away, but I personally never saw quite such a fine collection of scrap iron again.

Reverting to the subject of prangs, there were two in particular which I recall very vividly, probably because I was slightly involved in them.

Asymmetric overshoots

One was a kite belonging to "B" flight, which pranged when doing a three-engined overshoot. This was undoubtedly the most frequent source of mishaps, particularly after we received Hercs, with their greater power. When opening up on three engines it was essential to have the one engine considerably in advance of the other two, and correct the tendency to drop a wing and swing with rudder and aileron as the other two came up to full power. If all three were opened up together, the aircraft would swing towards the stopped engine, and the wing dropped before corrective action could take effect. As overshoots were usually done from an altitude of 100ft or less, the aircraft frequently hit the deck at an angle to the runway on one wheel and possibly a wing tip, and went careering across the aerodrome until it either just stopped or the long-suffering undercarriage collapsed and the aircraft came to a "grinding 'alt."

In this particular instance, the kite came bouncing across the aerodrome on a wheel and a wing tip, heading straight for a parked aircraft which

was being worked on. I was standing on one side of the dispersal and saw it coming, so I yelled to the other blokes, who scrambled down the engine trestles, tumbled out of the aircraft, and evacuated the vicinity at high speed. For some odd reason, however, I remained rooted to the spot, watching the aircraft bounding towards me like some huge prehistoric monster intent on its prey. The starboard wing-tip hit the ground ten feet, (we measured it afterwards) from the port fin of the parked aircraft. The next bounce should have taken her smack on to the port wing of the stationary Halifax.

However, for some extraordinary reason she bounced off to port, and missing the other machine, ploughed into the young fir trees at the side of the dispersal and stopped, with her undercarriage collapsed and her back broken. Two engines were torn out, and the reduction gear came off a third, which caught fire. I rushed across the dispersal and saw the emergency hatch above the cockpit open, and the crew start emerging with undignified haste, which seemed to be a very satisfactory state of affairs.

I wondered about the rear gunner, and ran down to the rear turret to have a look. The gunner was still sitting in his turret, not quite unconscious, but dazed and silly, not knowing where he was and caring even less. I grabbed my screwdriver from the rule pocket of my overalls, where we always carried them, and smashed a hole in the perspex, put my arm in and moved the emergency control to "Free". This enabled me to swing the turret round in order to get at the doors. At this moment another chap arrived to help, and we reached up, opened them, grabbed the gunner's shoulders and started to pull him out backwards, this being the normal method of exit from a turret. As he felt himself going, he grabbed at something in the turret and hung on like a limpet.

This incurred my severe displeasure, as I was by now absolutely terrified

by the crackling of the fire, the smell of petrol and hot engines, and the smoke from the bomb bay, where some small practice bombs had gone off. There was I, expecting to be blown to eternity by the tanks exploding at any moment and to get a posthumous George Medal, or at least a mention in despatches for my rescue (or attempted rescue), and the silly clot didn't *want* to be rescued! However, there was no time to argue if I was going to collect the "gong" in person, so we both heaved, and he came out of the turret like a cork out of a bottle, knocking us both flat on our backs. We picked ourselves up, half carried and half dragged him to a reasonably safe distance, and then turned and surveyed the scene.

It was most disappointing. Some intelligent characters were playing fire extinguishers on the dying embers of the fire, which they had prevented from spreading, and with the fire died our hopes of glory!

Actually, had the aircraft pranged anywhere except just on the edge of a dispersal, where there were always several fire extinguishers kept handy, the results would not have been so funny, and even as it was, they could easily have been very different.

A losing battle

The other prang that I particularly remember was one of our own aircraft, "R" Robert. One evening, about six o'clock, I was refuelling an aircraft on a dispersal about 100 yards from the upwind end of one of the short runways, which happened to be the one in use. I had just returned from tea for night flying, and there was only one more kite to come in from day flying—"R" Robert. I heard engines suddenly being opened up and, looking down the runway, saw a "Halibag" at about 20ft, obviously intending to overshoot. The engines did not seem to be at full power and, as I watched, instead of the flaps going up, the bomb doors opened.

This was a bit unorthodox, to say the least, and I watched him, hoping

that he was not going to swing my way, as I was standing on top of a lot of petrol, with a lot more in the bowser ten yards away. After staggering three-quarters of the length of the runway the kite decided to take matters into her own hands and plonked down on her long-suffering undercarriage. She shot off the end of the runway, ran about 50 yards into a potato field, sank in up to the axles, stood on her nose, broke her back just behind the cockpit, and flopped down again, the port undercarriage giving up the struggle as she did so.

I nipped down from the wing and galloped across, accompanied by the other boys, but by the time we got there everyone was out and waiting for the blood wagon to give them a ride back to the tech. site. This they earned, for when the ambulance and crash tender arrived both became bogged down, and the crew helped us man-handle them back to *terra firma*.

Subsequently the story came out. Having throttled back to land, the silly clot had engaged the friction lock, designed to prevent the throttle settings from varying in flight owing to vibration. He then decided that he was too high and would have to overshoot. To this end he pushed at the throttle levers, and after a struggle got them up to about half power. He then thought that he ought to get the flaps up, which was a reasonable thing to do, but in a Halifax the flap lever is adjacent to the bomb door lever, the flap lever moving up to raise the flaps, and the bomb door lever up to open the bomb doors. Needless to say, he grabbed the wrong lever, and in-

stead of reducing drag by raising the flaps, he increased it by opening the bomb doors.

Hard labour

Unfortunately for us this was only the beginning, for having finished our interrupted refuelling, we returned to the flight office to await the arrival of the night flying aircrews for the three kites that were on cross-countries that night. Flying control rang up and said that while they would let the aircraft take off, they would not allow them to land, as the wreck was in line with the runway. Would we therefore please remove it before 2.30 a.m., when the kites were due back?

Just as easy as that!

We rang up and had the station duty crew organise some equipment and some transport to bring it out. We saw the kites off, had a quick supper sent out by the cookhouse, and got cracking at about eight o'clock.

The first thing to do was jack up the port wing with a device known as a "trac-jac", consisting of a padded cradle and a hydraulic jack mounted on four caterpillar wheels. The snag was that as the wing tip was buried, and the starboard main wheel bogged

down. The wing was too low to get the trac-jac underneath it, so we lay on our faces under the wing and dug a pit about a foot deep to make the extra height. We then manœuvred the jack into position and started pumping. Unfortunately, instead of the aircraft going up, the jack started going down into the mud. We heaved it out and man-handled some "de-bogging boards" into position for the jack to stand on. These boards were about 12ft long and three feet wide, made out of two-inch thick timber with a solid angle-iron frame, and weighed perhaps a couple of hundredweight.

We then discovered that, owing to their thickness, the jack would not go under again, so we had to hump them out and do some more digging, but eventually we got the boards and the jack in position. We then jacked the kite up, so that it could be moved. Next we had to dig a sloping ramp down to the bottom of the starboard wheel, surfacing it with de-bogging boards, and do the same for the tail wheel, which had disappeared completely so that the bottom of the rear fuselage was resting on the mud.

By about 1.30 a.m. we were just about to start moving, with the aid of a Bowser winching on the starboard

wheel, another on the trac-jac, and a tractor on the tail wheel, when a member of the duty crew, whom we had borrowed to act as a telephone orderly, came down from the office and told us that Control had just rung up and said that as they were expecting fog, they were diverting the aircraft to another station, so we need not worry about moving the wreck..!

After a brief interlude, during which many varied aspersions were cast upon Flying Control's ancestors and descendants, we decided that having got so far, we might as well finish the adjectival job. We made slow progress, having to keep relaying the de-bogging boards as we went, and finally got her back on to the peri-track about 2.30. As we turned her, the nose section which, owing to her broken back, had been dragging along the ground retained only by a few wires and pipes etc., fell off completely. We left it there until we had parked the rest of the aircraft on a dispersal, and then we picked it up with a crane, dumped it on a couple of trolleys and wheeled it away. As the kites had been diverted, we then called it a night, and finally crawled back to the billet and bed at about 4.30 a.m., rather the worse for wear.

Had the aircraft travelled a further 100 yards beyond where she pranged, she would have finished up in some greenhouses in which little seemed to be grown *except* Halifaxes. Periodically a kite would prang in them, they would just about be replaced, and a crop of tomatoes or something coming along nicely, when another Halifax would knock them down again. This, so I was told, had been going on for several years. I imagine the proprietor had them well insured, and in any case he could claim from the Air Ministry, so I should think he did quite well from his crop of Halifaxes.

Flight

The Halifax's leading lady

During World War Two LETTICE CURTIS ferried 222 Handley Page Halifax bombers for the Air Transport Auxiliary. She recalls here how she became the first woman licensed to fly four-engined RAF aircraft

AN acute shortage of trained pilots in 1941 and yet another threat of invasion, brought to the women of the Air Transport Auxiliary (ATA), their greatest ever challenge. The ever-increasing numbers of new aircraft coming off the production lines finally persuaded the powers that be in the RAF to allow the women of the ATA to share with their male colleagues, in the ferrying of operational aircraft.

At first, it was only the single-engined Hurricanes and Spitfires that they were allowed to fly, but as the year wore on, operational twins such as the Blenheim, Hampden and Wellington were, for a selected few, added to the list. Meanwhile, the number of new four-engined bombers was also rising, until by mid-1942, some 150 a month were leaving the factories. At this stage these aircraft were principally Halifaxes, since the Lancaster, which had been developed from the twin-engined Manchester, was not yet being produced in sizeable quantities, and the Stirling bomber was having operational prob-

lems. To cope with the movement of these aircraft, it was decided that the time had now come to supplement the ATA's Flying Training School at White Waltham with some formal training for the conversion of pilots from twin to four-engined types. In fact the ATA had tried to do this once before, and they had earmarked for the task, a Focke-Wulf Condor which a Danish airline pilot, Capt Hansen, had brought with him when he escaped to Britain. The aircraft had, however, run into maintenance problems and, in any case, had been written off shortly afterwards as a result of overshooting whilst landing on wet grass.

At much the same time the Ministry of Aircraft Production (MAP) had agreed to some proposals for training RAF 41 Group test pilots on "multis." Since it was necessary for a training aircraft to be based at an airfield where it could be maintained, MAP had allotted a Liberator at Prestwick, a Fortress at Burtonwood, a Halifax at Leavesden and a Stirling at Hull-avington. It was arranged that 41

Group would provide their own instructors. During the summer of 1942, the ATA sent a limited number of pilots to Prestwick and Burton-wood, for some solo practice. This came to an end when, in the autumn of that year, the ATA took over control of the Leavesden Halifax, BD.191—an early Mark II version that had seen better days. The instructor delegated to take charge of ATA training was pre-war LOT pilot Capt Klemens Dlugaszewski. He had joined the Polish airline at its inception in 1929 and must have been one of the most experienced pilots flying with the ATA. As Leavesden consisted of only one 1,000yd runway which sloped significantly at one end, it was not in itself a suitable place for training. The routine therefore was for "Dluga" to fly the flight engineer and two, or possibly three, pupils to Leavesden in an Anson. On arrival he would telephone nearby RAF stations with a runway suitably into wind, to seek permission to use it for a limited number of circuits.

The ATA ferry pools responsible for moving the bulk of the Halifaxes were No 1 FPP, White Waltham, which cleared the Handley Page parent factory at Radlett and that of the London Aircraft Production group

Heading picture, *Halifax II W7773 photographed in July 1942.* **Inset,** *the author in the left hand seat of a Halifax.* **Right,** *this series of photographs was taken from Halifax II JP193 on January 6, 1944 during a landing approach into Leavesden. The pilot was T. W. Morton. Note the Leavesden-built Mosquitoes awaiting collection by the ATA in the* **bottom photograph.**

E. J. Riding photos

at Leavesden, and No 14 FPP at Ringway, Manchester. The latter had in its parish the factories of sub-contractors Rootes Securities at Speke, English Electric at Preston and Fairey Aviation at Ringway. With the expansion of bomber output, these two ferry pools had priority for additional four-engined ferry pilots. No 14 FPP at Ringway was one of only three ATA ferry pools that throughout the war, never had female pilots attached to them. This put me in a fortunate position as at that time I was one of only two women pilots attached to No 1 ferry pool and so the chances of flying four-engined aircraft were much greater.

I had gone there at my own request in May 1942, from the all-women ferry pool at Hamble. The vast majority of ferry tasks at Hamble consisted of short Spitfire deliveries from south coast Spitfire factories to such places as Lyneham, Brize Norton and Little Rissington. Aircraft that had to go any distance north had usually to be handed over to the White Waltham ferry pool for onward ferrying, since this reduced the length of time a pilot was away from base, and also cut down on what might otherwise have been long taxi journeys. A further disadvantage was that there were only a limited number of twin-engined aircraft to be ferried from the Hamble area and these had to be shared out amongst a number of qualified pilots. At White Waltham there was a much greater range of aircraft to ferry and longer trips; it was also a much larger ferry pool. In addition White Waltham was the home of ATA Headquarters and the main training base and as such, was the focal point of the whole organisation. Everyone in the ATA came to White Waltham at some time and all this, in my book, built up to more variety and a greater challenge.

I had been accepted into No 1 FPP on the understanding that I was to be treated on an entirely equal basis with the men. To prove myself, I had gone out of my way to take on rather more than my fair share of ferry trips, on all types of single and twin-engined aircraft including the unpopular ones such as the Beaufort

and Tomahawk. Candidates for four-engine training or "Class 5" as the ATA termed it, were selected by ferry pool Commanders. Thanks to an exceptionally fair-minded, and un-biased CO, my diligence paid off and on September 24, 1942, I found myself posted to the school for a four-engine training course which involved flying the Halifax based at Leavesden. At virtually any other ferry pool an opportunity like this for a female would, quite simply, never have arisen. On the following day I handled the aircraft for the first time in the air, en route to Bassingbourn where another pilot did some circuits. The next day I did 35min dual which included two landings. I found that the aircraft was definitely heavier on the controls than anything I had flown before, especially on the ailerons, and that the cockpit was quite a bit higher off the ground. It was also a good deal heavier weight-wise and, as such, was less manœuvrable at normal control loads.

Due to bad weather and the aircraft being out of service, it was a week before I flew again; this time for 40min. Then on October 6 I got a morning of tuition to myself and put in 1hr 20min. Thus in my first fortnight I had achieved no more than a

Halifax II Series I Special, BB324 of No 10 Sqn, with faired nose and with dorsal turret deleted.

scrappy $2\frac{1}{2}$hr. The last two flights had been from Bovingdon, but on October 11, which was the next day we flew, we took the aircraft to Hampstead Norris on the hills west of Reading and after this flight, "Dluga" declared me ready for solo flight. He was not, however, prepared to let me do my first solo flight from the comparatively short runway available there and it was over two weeks before aircraft serviceability and suitable weather coincided again. Only another pilot, I think, can understand the unsettlement and heart-searchings that these continual breaks in training engendered. Also, my pride was taking a severe denting by the seemingly long time I was taking to get cleared. "Dluga" had, of course, been given strict instructions to be even more careful than usual before clearing me—or even letting me go solo—and the weather and unserviceability of the aircraft had helped neither him, nor me.

I felt that I was letting down my ferry pool CO who had had the courage to recommend me and also the women pilots who, if I failed, might not be given a second chance. I felt too that the whole affair was playing into the hands of a few White Waltham "oldies" who, nodding their heads knowingly, inferred even if they did not actually say it that it was ridiculous to expect women to be able to cope with these aircraft.

But even worse was to come morale-wise. On Monday, October 26, Mrs Roosevelt, who was on a "hustle tour" of this country, came to White Waltham with Mrs Churchill, to meet senior ATA officers and in particular, to visit a selection of the American women pilots who were flying with the ATA. Inevitably, as this was a publicity exercise, the Press were present and although I had not even gone solo, the headlines next day shouted "Mrs Roosevelt Meets Halifax Girl Pilot." What ignominy if I should fail now!

Luckily, on the very next day the Halifax was once more in business, and after a break of 16 days and a couple more circuits, I finally solo-ed. The first hurdle had been crossed and for a brief moment, I had a welcome feeling of achievement. Four days later I carried out a further six solo circuits. This time Jim Bain, the ATA's senior flight engineer flew with me in order to counter any opposition from other flight engineers about flying with me—one flight engineer being the only crew we carried. At this point problems of aircraft serviceability, November weather and not least that of finding a suitable field to fly from, brought the training scheme to a halt. Two hours solo with seven landings would have been more than adequate to clear a male pilot, but I found myself being posted back to No 1 ferry pool still only cleared

to fly singles and twins. Nobody explained why. To have got so far and not made it was, at the least, a bitter disappointment. In later years I was to be told that the ATA school's CFI had made an arbitrary rule that I must do ten solo landings before being let loose on ferrying. In retrospect, however, the decision may not have been all bad. There were problems enough in coping with the bad weather and short days of winter in aircraft to which one was accustomed. Anyway, by the end of November yet another scheme had been devised for training ATA and No 41 Group pilots. On November 26 the establishment of No 1475 (Halifax) Training Flight was approved. This was to be formed at the RAF bomber station of Pocklington, which was 12 miles east of York.

Posted to Pocklington

The ATA instructor posted to the flight was Capt R. H. Henderson who had been acting as test pilot to the ATA's technical department which prepared much-needed "Pilot's Notes." It had been arranged that he was to share the task of running the flight with a Squadron Leader from No 41 Group who would be in charge of the RAF maintenance personnel. The day after Henderson's arrival, however, the Squadron Leader was posted, leaving him in the unusual position for a civilian, of being in sole charge of some 30 RAF fitters and riggers and the No 41 Group NCOs. Early in February 1943, I was posted to Pocklington to continue with my four-engined training.

It had been arranged that whilst I was there, I would live with the WAAF Officers who, in those days, were not allowed to use the main Officer's Mess—at bomber stations anyway. So I had to return to the "WAAFery" not only at night, but for all my meals. Except when actually flying therefore, I had no contact with other male trainees and in the evening, instead of flying talk, I had to listen to endless chat about local boyfriends, in which I could not join. This both depressed me and made me feel out of place. I would have been happier staying in a local pub, but this was ruled out on the grounds of transport problems.

For the first week the weather was against me once more and I flew only once. When we finally got going, thankfully I went solo almost right away. The aircraft we used were again very early versions of the Mark II (W.1005, R.9389) because at this juncture in the war bombers were at a premium. They were equipped with high frequency radio-telephones with distinctly poor reception, and even during training flights the aircraft were armed and carried air gunners.

The training itself, organised on more formal lines than at Leavesden, was based on standard RAF details. In retrospect, I feel that "Hendy" must have received special instructions to make quite sure that I was strong enough to cope under adverse conditions, for we certainly did an abnormal number of three-engined, two-engined and cross-wind landings which gave rise, I recall, to some fairly hectic moments. The Halifax around this time had been the subject of a number of unexplained accidents in which aircraft had "gone in" on the approach. This was later attributed to fin stall and rudder overbalance, and redesigned fins were fitted during the year as a retrospective modification. Because of this, pilots were warned to avoid violent manoeuvres—something which in any case I would have been most unlikely to attempt, for it was always my instinct to avoid situations from which the only way out was use of brute force. To those who say that the aircraft was far too heavy for women to fly, I would say that of course, if one was unlucky, conditions might arise in which one might be unable to cope, but the margin between this and a situation in which a man could not cope either, was a small one. The times when a man could have saved the situation by virtue of extra physical strength must have been few and far between. Foresight and good anticipation are far more important qualities.

The course closed with some final cross-wind landings on February 25 and I returned to White Waltham, without even a small celebration. It was usual for the Operations staff at ferry pools to arrange for a pilot returning from a course, to be given a straightforward ferry trip as soon as possible on the new type for which they had been cleared. Thus two days later when Rear Admiral Boucher, who commanded the ATA Northern Area from Prestwick, was required to come south on duty, it was arranged that he should leave his Halifax at Mount Farm, a runwayed airfield just over the hills from White Waltham. I would then take it over at Mount Farm and ferry it to its destination. Thus my first Halifax ferry trip, on February 27, 1943, was in a Rootes-built Mk V version, DG.303, from Mount Farm to the undulating grass airfield at Netheravon where it was delivered to 295 Sqn, for use in connection with the movement of airborne troops.

Between 1940 and 1945 the ATA delivered 9,326 Halifaxes and of these, I ferried 222. Ten other women were eventually cleared for four-engined flying and all (except Joan Hughes, who was trained on the Stirling) did their conversion courses at Marston Moor where, barely two weeks after I had left, No 1475 (Halifax) Training Flight had moved. Here it amalgamated with the Bomber Command Training Flight until in May it was finally disbanded and the training of ATA and 41 Group pilots was taken over by Bomber Command. For the ATA, four-engined training had at last become a matter of routine.

Pssst! wanna buy a secondhand bomber?

It is a sad fact that of the 6,176 Halifax bombers built during the period 1939-46 only one substantially complete example, W1048, in the RAF Bomber Command Museum at Hendon, survives today. Yet after the war there were no less than 161 Halifaxes on the British civil aircraft register, many of them serving as a stopgap for the late arrival of the new, post-war generation of airliners.

More than half of those Halifaxes allocated civil registrations were never used in a civilian capacity and were destined to be cannibalised to keep their brethren airborne.

The first civil Halifax conversion was a Mk 3, NR169. This aircraft became G-AGXA and, named *Waltzing Matilda*, was flown to Australia in May 1946. This journey was described by the pilot Geoffrey Wikner in the September 1979 issue of *Aeroplane Monthly*.

When, in 1945, a number of Halifax C Mk 8 transports came up for disposal, large numbers were snapped up by London Aero and Motor Services, BOAC and the Lancashire Aircraft Corporation Ltd. A total of 80 C Mk 8s was registered, out of 96 built, and they were used for a variety of tasks, many eventually being employed on the Berlin Airlift. The first C Mk 8, PP217, was first flown in June 1945. The dorsal turrets were deleted and fairings replaced the tail turrets. Eleven passengers were carried, plus 8,000lb of freight in detachable belly panniers. The C Mk 8 was powered by four 1,675 h.p. Bristol Hercules XVI engines.

In time there was a shortage of spares for these hardworked aircraft but, fortunately, during 1947-48, 31 Halifax B Mk 6s were released from the RAF. The Mk 6 Halifax had additional tankage and extended wingtips. The first production aircraft, NP715, was first flown on October 10, 1945. The power was supplied by four 1,800 h.p. Bristol Hercules 100s. Most of those allocated for civil use were used for spares, their one and only flight

Heading photograph. *Halifax C Mk 8 PP311 with roundels painted out and the civil registration G-AHYI applied just forward of the tailplane. This aircraft was registered to BOAC in September 1946 but was returned to the RAF as PP311 in July 1947. In January 1948 it was registered again, this time to Anglo French Distributors Ltd, and was delivered to Gatwick with daubed civil markings. In March 1949 'HYI was bought by Skyflight Ltd but was scrapped the same year.*

in civil markings being made from various MUs to either Stansted or Bovingdon, where they were invariably broken up.

During 1948 the airfreight business began to tail off and the Halifax's future as a civil transport became uncertain. And then came the Berlin Airlift in June 1948, which saved many Halifaxes from the

Bottom, *Halifax B Mk 6 RG785 was registered in November 1947 to London Aero Motor Services Ltd and delivered to Stansted still in its RAF marks. The marks G-AJBE were probably never worn, though a Piper Cub was given the same registration in April 1947. RG785 was sold to the Pakistan Air Force in October 1949.*

Right, *Halifax B Mk 6 ST801 photographed at Southend in 1949 wearing the marks G-ALOM. Though registered to Aviation Traders Ltd the Halifax was reduced to spares in November 1949.*

Lower right, *Halifax C Mk 8 PP329 awaiting conversion in 1948. The code letters GR-P are still visible denoting that the aircraft is a 301 (Polish) Squadron Halifax. Registered G-AKBR this aircraft had several owners and flew on the Berlin Airlift with Skyflight Ltd from September 1948. After this it was sold to Eagle Aviation Ltd in August 1949 and scrapped the following year.*

scrapman's melting pot for at least a further year. Every airworthy Halifax was pressed into round-the-clock service from Schleswigland and Wunsdorf into Gatow, seven companies operating a total of 41 Halifaxes. When the 'lift ended in August 1949 so ended the Halifax's career as a civil aeroplane. Those that were not scrapped were sold abroad.

In addition to the Mk 6s and Mk 8s already mentioned a large batch of Halifax A Mk 9s was registered in 1949-50. The Halifax A Mk 9 had superseded the A III and A VII, and entered service with RAF Transport Command in 1946. It was produced for the Airborne Forces, could carry 12 paras and was equipped for glider towing. Powered by four 1,675 h.p. Hercules XVIs, a total of 145 had been built when orders for further aircraft were cancelled. A total of 32 A Mk 9s was registered, most of them to Aviation Traders Ltd at Southend who promptly disposed of them to the Egyptian Air Force early in 1950.

Most of the aircraft featured here were never converted for civilian use—their large hulks remaining dotted around Southend, Stansted and elsewhere until the scrapman's blowtorch had done its work.

Right, *Halifax C Mk 8 PP317 was registered to BOAC in September 1946 and transferred back to the RAF in April 1947. In January 1948 it was restored to the register to Anglo French Distributors Ltd.*

Below, *Halifax C Mk 8 PP324 waiting in vain for conversion for civil use. The 301 (Polish) Squadron markings GR-V are still visible. Registered G-AKGO this Halifax was registered to Airtech Ltd and delivered to Stansted still in RAF markings in May 1948, but was never converted.*

Right, *Halifax A Mk 9 RT846 originally served with 1 FU. After disposal from the RAF it was registered G-ALOP to Aviation Traders at Southend. In February it was ferried to the Egyptian Air Force with the Arabic serial number 1155.*

A. J. Jackson collection

Right, *Halifax A Mk 9 RT888 served with 1 FU and then the MEDME before being acquired by Aviation Traders and registered G-ALOR in April 1949. This too was delivered to the Egyptian Air Force in February 1950. EAF serial number was 1157.*

A. J. Jackson collection

Right, *Halifax A Mk 9 RT937 seen at Southend with the temporary registration letters G-ALOS. On the fin is painted Lot 145. Lot 145 eventually flew on the Berlin Airlift with Bond Air Services and was later scrapped.*

Bottom, *Halifax A Mk 9 RT787 served with 1361 Flt before passing on to Nos 521 and 518 Squadrons. After disposal from the RAF RT787 was registered G-ALOO and sold to the Egyptian Air Force via Aviation Traders Ltd in February 1950. The EAF serial number was 1158.*

A. J. Jackson collection

69

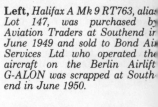

Left, *Halifax A Mk 9 RT763, alias Lot 147, was purchased by Aviation Traders at Southend in June 1949 and sold to Bond Air Services Ltd who operated the aircraft on the Berlin Airlift. G-ALON was scrapped at Southend in June 1950.*

A. J. Jackson collection

Left, *Halifax A Mk 9 RT87 served with 47 Squadron, and on disposal from the RAF was acquired by Aviation Traders Ltd and delivered to Southend in night camouflage and white lettering. It was scrapped there in January 1950.*

A. J. Jackson collection

Another Halifax A Mk 9 destined for the Egyptian Air Force was RT793, seen here at Southend before delivery in January 1950. Previously RT793 served with Nos 47 and 113 Squadrons before moving to 1332 HTCU.

Bottom, *Halifax C Mk 8 PP24 was registered G-AIWR to London Aero Motor Services (South Africa) Ltd but soon took up South African markings ZS-BUL for operating pilgrim flights between Istanbul, Nairobi and Jeddah. Its short civil life came to an end at Port Sudan after a crash landing in November 1947.*

A. J. Jackson collection

The Aeroplane

A BROOKLANDS AIRCRAFT PORTFOLIO

Boeing B-17 and B-29
FORTRESS and SUPERFORTRESS
PORTFOLIO

A BROOKLANDS AIRCRAFT PORTFOLIO

A BROOKLANDS AIRCRAFT PORTFOLIO

De Havilland

MOSQUITO

PORTFOLIO

One of a series comprising technical descriptions—cutaway drawings— genealogy—combat and operational reports from contemporary articles from Flight, The Aeroplane and Aircraft Production, with modern material from *AEROPLANE*

De Havilland
MOSQUITO
PORTFOLIO